PRAISE FOR *SECOND CHANCE*

"In his compelling new book . . . Mr. Brzezinski not only assesses the short- and long-term fallout of the Iraq war, but also puts that grim situation in perspective . . . [Brzezinski] writes with a keen understanding of the ways in which military or political actions in one part of the world can affect developments in another region . . . Mr. Brzezinski's verdict on the current president's record—'catastrophic,' he calls it—is nothing short of devastating."

—MICHIKO KAKUTANI, *New York Times*

"In his engaging and briskly argued new book, Jimmy Carter's national security adviser sees little worth emulating in the past 15 years of U.S. foreign policy . . . What *Second Chance* does offer is a wise insight that should guide any effort to fashion a strategy to restore American leadership."

—JAMES M. LINDSAY, *Washington Post* Book World

"Carter's great accomplishment was to put human rights at the center of American foreign policy, and it is here that Brzezinski is at his best . . . Brzezinski covers a great deal of ground with dispatch and verve."

—*New York Times* Book Review

"Brzezinski has written a short critique of U.S. foreign policy since 1991, but it merits careful and considered reflection.

Historians, in particular, should welcome his contribution, as he affirms the value of historical reasoning for understanding complex international realities while critiquing more sweeping theoretical approaches . . . Yet by calling for a 'historically relevant vision' to guide U.S. foreign policy, Brzezinski redefines 'realism' in a way that confirms history—rather than theory—as the best guide to action."

—*New Global Studies*, International Security
Studies Program, Yale University

SECOND CHANCE

Three Presidents
and the Crisis of
American Superpower

ZBIGNIEW BRZEZINSKI

BASIC
BOOKS

A Member of the Perseus Books Group
New York

The Library of Congress has catalogued the hardcover edition as follows:

Brzezinski, Zbigniew.
    Second chance : three presidents and the crisis of American superpower /
Zbigniew Brzezinski.
        p. cm.
    Includes index.
    ISBN-13: 978-0-465-00252-8 (alk. paper)
    ISBN-10: 0-465-00252-8 (alk. paper)
        1. United States—Foreign relations—1989-. 2. Bush, George, 1924-.
3. Clinton, Bill, 1946-. 4. Bush, George W. (George Walker), 1946-. I. Title.

JZ1480.B69 2007
327.73—dc22
                                                                2006039290

ISBN (PB): 978-0-465-00355-6
10 9 8 7 6 5 4 3 2

Contents

1

The Challenge of
Global Leadership

THE SELF-CORONATION OF THE U.S. PRESIDENT AS the first Global Leader was a moment in historical time if not a specific date on the calendar. It followed the collapse of the Soviet Union and the end of the Cold War. The American president simply began to act as the global leader without any official international blessing. The American media proclaimed him as such, foreigners deferred to him, and a visit to the White House (not to mention Camp David) became the high point in any foreign leader's political life. Presidential travels abroad assumed the trappings of imperial expeditions, over-shadowing in scale and security demands the circumstances of any other statesman.

This de facto coronation was less imposing and yet more consequential than its closest historic precedent, Queen Victoria's designation by the British Parliament in 1876 as empress of India. Proclaimed in a glittering ceremony in New Delhi a year later, attended (in the words of the official announcement) by India's "princes, chiefs, and nobles in whose persons the antiquity of the past is associated with the prosperity of the present, and who so worthily contribute to the splendor and stability of this great empire," the event symbolized Great Britain's unique worldwide status. "The sun never sets on the British empire" was henceforth the proud refrain of the loyal servants of the first global imperium.

Alas, the faithful courtiers underestimated how very fickle history can be. Guided more by imperial hubris than by a historically relevant vision, the British empire in less than a quarter of a century became embroiled in a self-destructive far-away conflict. The two successive Boer Wars (which discredited the "liberal" British empire, gave Hitler the model for concentration camps, saw the rendition of prisoners to confinement in distant British-held islands, and plunged the conventional British army into protracted guerrilla warfare) left the imperial homeland politically split and financially strained. Two devastating and draining world wars followed, and before long the great empire became a mere junior partner of its successor, the United States of America.

America's anointment as the world's leader is in some respects reminiscent of Napoleon's self-coronation. Napoleon, who grasped the imperial crown from papal hands and placed it on his own head, saw himself as history's personal agent, channeling the revolutionary awakening of the French masses into a grand reconstruction of Europe. *Liberté, Fraternité,*

Egalité were to be shared forcefully with all Europeans, whether they desired it or not. A decade or so after the self-coronation of the first American global leader, a U.S. president, not unlike Napoleon, was proclaiming that America's historical mission (and his own) is to spur the transformation of no less than the culture and politics of the entire world of Islam. The new century, it seemed, was America's and now it was America's task to shape it.

Symptomatic of the first decade and a half of America's supremacy were the worldwide presence of U.S. military forces and the increased frequency of their engagement in combat or coercive operations. Deployed on every continent and dominating every ocean, the United States had no political or military peer. Every other power was essentially regional. And one way or another, most countries of the world had to live with U.S. ground or naval forces nearby. (See Figure 1.)

In history, fifteen years is a mere episode, but we live at a time when history accelerates at a pace unimaginable even a few decades ago. It is therefore not too early to undertake a strategic appraisal of America's international performance since its emergence around 1990 as the world's only superpower. Never before in history has a single power been so paramount. Whether America has been exercising its international leadership responsibly and effectively is therefore a vital question not only for the security and well-being of Americans but also the world at large.

Beyond the obvious requirement of protecting its own national security, America's emergence as the world's most powerful state has saddled Washington's leadership with three central missions:

FIGURE 1 ❖ POST-COLD WAR U.S.

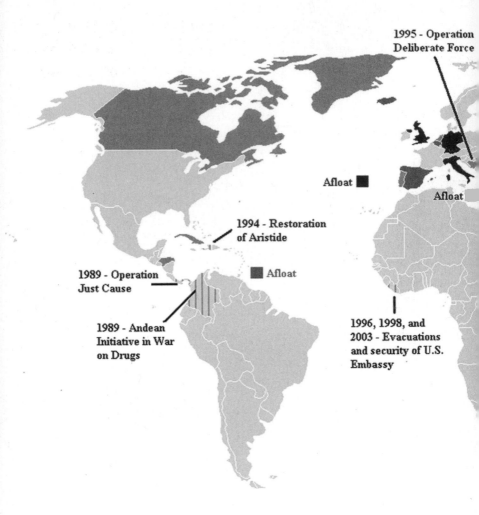

1995 - Operation
Deliberate Force

Afloat ■

Afloat

1994 - Restoration
of Aristide

1989 - Operation
Just Cause

■ Afloat

1989 - Andean
Initiative in War
on Drugs

1996, 1998, and
2003 - Evacuations
and security of U.S.
Embassy

Prepared by Thomas Williams and Brett Edkins

MILITARY OPERATIONS AND DEPLOYMENT

Major combat, paramilitary, or peacekeeping operation

10,000+ troops

1,000+ troops

100+ troops

1999 - Operation Allied Force

1991 - Operations Desert Shield and Desert Fox
1998 - Operation Desert Fox
2003 - Operation Iraqi Freedom

2001 - Operation Enduring Freedom

1995 – 1996 – Taiwan Straits Crisis

1998 - Operation Infinite Reach

Afloat

Afloat

1992 – 1995 – Operation Restore Hope

1. To manage, steer, and shape central power relationships in a world of shifting geopolitical balances and intensifying national aspirations so that a more cooperative global system can emerge.

2. To contain or terminate conflicts, prevent terrorism and the proliferation of weapons of mass destruction, and promote collective peacekeeping in regions torn by civil strife so that global violence recedes rather than spreads.

3. To address more effectively the increasingly intolerable inequalities in the human condition, in keeping with the novel reality of an emerging "global conscience," and to prompt a common response to the new environmental and ecological threats to global well-being.

Each of these tasks was, and remains fifteen years later, monumental in scope. Together, they serve as the litmus test of America's ability to lead.

The enormity of this historical test necessarily leads to a more pointed inquiry: how did America's first three global leader presidents—George H. W. Bush, William J. Clinton, and George W. Bush—interpret the essence of the new era? Were they guided by a historically relevant vision, and did they pursue a coherent strategy? Which foreign policy decisions were the most consequential? Did they leave the world in better or worse shape, and was the American position in that world stronger or weaker? And what key lessons for the future should be drawn from America's performance over the past fifteen years as the first global superpower?

One superpower, fifteen years, three presidents: that in a nutshell is the focus of this book.

But the appraisal that follows is not only a critique. In addition to dissecting sins of omission and commission, the book postulates certain basic strategic conclusions and fundamental guidelines regarding the current moment in history that ought to enlighten future American presidents. Even the world's paramount superpower can go badly astray and endanger its own primacy if its strategy is misguided and its understanding of the world is faulty.

Moreover, Americans need to ask themselves whether American society is guided by values, and its government structured in a manner, congenial to effective long-term global leadership. And do they understand the historical moment in which their country finds itself acting as global leader? These vital questions are addressed in the concluding chapter, following the critical review of the record. That chapter draws lessons from the recent past, speculates as to what might have been, and postulates the basic principles that should guide America if it is to succeed in fulfilling its historical vocation.

This book is thus a subjective statement. It is not a detailed history, though it reviews the historical record to extract pertinent answers to the above questions. As a personal appraisal, it also draws on my experience in policy making and in commenting on international affairs as an engaged observer. It reflects some of my past judgments but also revises them in the light of experience.

Though this book provides a critical assessment of America's accomplishments as well as failures in its new incarnation, it focuses particularly on the personal leadership of three presidents. In their new global role they both personify and epitomize America's special status in the contemporary world, and they alone make the ultimate decisions. But since presidential successes or failures are also America's successes or failures, the stakes involved are vastly greater than the individual records of this book's three central dramatis personae. Ultimately this discussion is about America's performance as global leader.

Leadership is partly a matter of character, partly intellect, partly organization, and partly what Machiavelli called "fortuna," the mysterious interaction of fate and chance. In the U.S. system, with its separation of powers, foreign policy is the area in which presidents have the greatest personal discretion. The glory, pomp, and power of the presidency are nowhere felt more strongly than in the arena of foreign affairs. Every president is captivated and enthralled by his unique possession of such special powers and by his unique access to information that no one else has. And there is a special allure to being a global statesman, especially to being the preeminent global statesman.

Yet presidents differ in their degree of personal involvement. Some, though they rarely say so, make foreign affairs their major preoccupation. These presidents tend to rely heavily on their national security advisers and elevate their importance. They are at the president's elbow, seeing him many times a day, and they help shape presidential perspectives. The National Security Council (NSC) therefore enjoys a special status in the White House as the president's executive arm in safeguarding the nation and dealing with the outside world.

Other presidents, who see domestic affairs as their central focus, tend to defer on foreign affairs to their secretaries of state. The secretary is thus delegated greater freedom of action in shaping policy and plays the role of primus inter pares on the president's foreign policy team. The national security adviser then becomes more of a staff director and a policy coordinator, while the president is more inclined to defer to the views of the secretary of state and his department. President Nixon and National Security Adviser Kissinger fell into the first category, with the NSC preeminent under direct presidential leadership, but President Ford and Secretary of State Kissinger fell into the second, with the State Department in the lead. President Carter (despite his initially limited experience in foreign affairs) was also in the first, thus elevating the NSC, while President Reagan, by appointing first General Alexander Haig and then George Shultz, clearly delegated much policy making to his secretary of state.

These are obviously not neat categories, but they help us broadly differentiate between different foreign policy-making styles. George H. W. Bush, the first global leader, came to office with considerable background in international affairs: a former head of the unofficial U.S. embassy in the People's Republic of China, U.N. ambassador, CIA director. He knew what he wanted to do, and he chose as his national security adviser an individual who shared his worldview, could serve as an experienced, effective alter ego, and was also a family friend.

Bill Clinton, the second global leader, had no experience in foreign affairs. He came to office with a vaguely formulated perspective on the new American role, and—as he stressed during his campaign—held the view that it was time to correct years of presidential neglect of America's domestic affairs. Foreign policy was initially of secondary importance, and thus in his first term neither of the two crucial foreign policy positions—national security adviser and secretary of state—was filled by an individual inclined to be strategically dominant.

During Clinton's second term, foreign policy clearly became more of a presidential preoccupation. Both key foreign policy positions were filled by more politically active figures, with the president himself more involved in foreign policy and not allowing either adviser to dominate. Strategic formulation suffered somewhat in that rather balanced arrangement, which fit neither of the two models of presidential leadership outlined above.

The third global leader, George W. Bush, was initially inclined to delegate foreign policy making to a distinguished national figure, a former general once widely considered an attractive presidential candidate. Bush thus seemed to fit the second model. But that did not last long. The events of 9/11, still within the first year of the first term, shook the president out of his foreign affairs lethargy. Policy then gravitated to the White House, to be dominated not by the national security adviser but by the vice president and a group of highly motivated officials in the White House and the Defense Department. They gained the president's ear and helped redefine him as the commander in chief of "a nation at war."

This pattern continued into Bush's second term. The replacement of the original secretary of state, Colin Powell, with Condoleezza Rice, the first term's national security adviser, enhanced the tactical role of the State Department in a decision-making structure still dominated on the strategic level by the same cluster of officials who had responded to 9/11 by infusing a personal sense of historic, almost religious mission into the president's role.

That, in broad strokes, is the bureaucratic context in which U.S. policy has been shaped since America's emergence as the world's preponderant state. The result has been a greatly enhanced presidency in the area of national security, with some serious and very contentious constitutional implications.

Each of the three presidents since America's victory in the Cold War has been the world's most important player in the world's most important game, and each has played in his own way. At this stage, suffice it to say that Global Leader I was the most experienced and diplomatically skillful but was not guided by any bold vision at a very unconventional historic moment. Global Leader II was the brightest and most futuristic, but he lacked strategic consistency in the use of American power. Global Leader III had strong gut instincts but no knowledge of global complexities and a temperament prone to dogmatic formulations.

The box below summarizes the fundamental changes in the global environment that occurred during the first decade and a half of America's unprecedented global primacy. These events are the basis on which the performance of the first three American global leaders will be appraised in the chapters that follow. The list shows, in capsule form, both the opportunities that were within America's reach and the steps leading to the increasingly complex crisis that superpower America now confronts.

TEN MAJOR TURNING POINTS, 1990–2006

Key developments reshaping the world system.

1. The Soviet Union is forced out of Eastern Europe and disintegrates. The United States is on top of the world.

2. The U.S. military victory in the first Gulf War is politically wasted. Middle Eastern peace is not pursued. Islamic hostility toward the United States begins to rise.

3. NATO and the European Union expand into Eastern Europe. The Atlantic community emerges as the predominant influence on the world scene.

4. Globalization is institutionalized with the creation of the World Trade Organization, the new role of the International Monetary Fund with its bailout fund, and the increased anticorruption agenda of the World Bank. "Singapore issues" become the foundation for the Doha Round of WTO negotiations.

5. The Asian financial crisis sets the foundation for a nascent East Asian regional community, to be characterized either by Chinese dominance or by Sino-Japanese competition. China's admission to the WTO encourages its ascent as a major global economic player and a center of regional trade agreements with politically more assertive and impatient poorer countries.

6. Two Chechen wars, the NATO conflict in Kosovo, and Vladimir Putin's election as president of Russia contribute to a rise in Russian authoritarianism and nationalism. Russia exploits its gas and oil resources to become an assertive energy superpower.

7. Facing a permissive attitude from the United States and others, India and Pakistan defy world public opinion to become nuclear powers. North Korea and Iran intensify their covert efforts to acquire nuclear capabilities in the face of inconsistent and inconsequential U.S. efforts to induce their self-restraint.

8. September 11, 2001, shocks the United States into a state of fear and the pursuit of unilateral policies. The United States declares war on terror.

9. The Atlantic community splits over the U.S. war in Iraq. The European Union fails to develop its own political identity or clout.

10. The post–1991 worldwide impression of U.S. global military omnipotence and Washington's illusions about the extent of America's power have been shattered by U.S. failures in postvictory Iraq. The United States acknowledges the need for cooperation with the European Union, China, Japan, and Russia regarding major issues of global security. The Middle East becomes the make-or-break test case of U.S. leadership.

DRAMATIS PERSONAE

(For reasons already explained, the three Presidents are mentioned by name in the chapters that follow, while their senior advisors are often referred to only by their specific functions, as listed below).

PRINCIPALS:

George H. W. Bush President of the United States   1989–1993
                    Global Leader I

Bill Clinton   President of the United States   1993–2001
                    Global Leader II

George W. Bush President of the United States   2001–
                    Global Leader III

KEY ADVISORS:

**Bush I
Administration**
                    National Security Advisor: **Brent Scowcroft**
                    1989–1993

                    Secretary of State: **James Baker**
                    1989–1992

                    Secretary of Defense: **Richard Cheney**
                    1989–1993

**Clinton
Administration**
                    National Security Advisor: **Anthony Lake**
                    1993–1997

                    Secretary of State: **Warren Christopher**
                    1993–1997

                    Secretary of Defense : **Les Aspin**
                    1993–1994

Secretary of Defense: **William Perry**
1994–1997

National Security Advisor: **Sandy Berger**
1997–2001

Secretary of State: **Madeleine Albright**
1997–2001

Secretary of Defense: **William Cohen**
1997–2001

**Bush II
Administration**

National Security Advisor: **Condoleezza Rice**
2001–2004

Secretary of State: **Colin Powell**
2001–2004

Secretary of Defense: **Donald Rumsfeld**
2001–2006

National Security Advisor: **Stephen Hadley**
2005–

Secretary of State: **Condoleezza Rice**
2005–

Secretary of Defense: **Robert Gates**
2006–

2

The Mists of Victory

(and the Spawning of
Clashing Historical Visions)

HISTORY CAN BE REDUCED TO FARCE, ESPECIALLY if it serves a political purpose. After the unexpectedly abrupt end of the Cold War, millions of Americans were repeatedly told that the defeat of Soviet communism was the doing of just one man. In its simplest rendering, this version of history could resemble a fairy tale, perhaps like this one:

> Once upon a time on Planet Earth there was an Evil Empire seeking global dominion. But when confronted by Ronald, the prince from the Republic of Freedom, the empire recoiled and before long, on December 26, 1991, its blood-stained red flag was lowered from the towering ramparts of the Kremlin castle. The Evil Empire had abjectly surrendered, and the Republic of Freedom lived happily ever after.

It was not quite so. A less romanticized account of what happened is the necessary point of departure for understanding the novel dilemmas America came to face—and had difficulty interpreting—in the wake of its sudden emergence as the world's only superpower.

The defeat of the Soviet Union was the consequence of a forty-year bipartisan effort that spanned the presidencies of Harry Truman, Dwight Eisenhower, John Kennedy, Lyndon Johnson, Richard Nixon, Gerald Ford, Jimmy Carter, Ronald Reagan, and George H. W. Bush. In different ways, almost every U.S. president made a substantial contribution to the outcome, but so did other figures, such as Pope John Paul II, Lech Walesa (the leader of the Polish Solidarity movement), and Mikhail Gorbachev (the initiator of the disruptive perestroika of the Soviet system).

John Paul II ignited a sense of spiritual vitality in politically suppressed Eastern Europe, revealing the hollowness of the decades-long communist indoctrination. Gorbachev, seeking a dynamic revival of the Soviet system, unintentionally brought to the surface the basic contradictions of bureaucratically sterile totalitarianism. Even worse for the tottering Soviet dictatorship, he permitted the rise of political dissent by eschewing Stalinist repression. The Solidarity movement in Poland successfully defied communist martial law for almost a decade and compelled a political compromise that ended the communist monopoly of power, which then precipitated upheavals in neighboring Czechoslovakia and Hungary, culminating in the collapse of the Berlin Wall.

Most importantly, several U.S. presidents shared a common understanding of the long-term threat posed by Soviet

U S.

communism. They deterred the Soviets from using military power to expand their dominion while forcing the rivalry into political and socioeconomic realms where the Soviet Union was at a disadvantage. Dwight Eisenhower enhanced the NATO alliance. John Kennedy defied the Kremlin's attempts to achieve a strategic breakthrough during both the Berlin and Cuban crises of the early 1960s. He also launched the dramatic race to the moon, which drained Soviet resources and deprived the Soviet Union of a potent ideological and political triumph. Recently opened Soviet archives reveal how intensely determined the Soviet leaders were to beat America in that race, how politically decisive they felt its outcome would be, and the extent to which America's success reversed the global post-Sputnik perception of Soviet technological superiority.

The failure of the American military effort in Vietnam and the resulting inclination to cut defense spending prompted President Nixon to seek détente with the Soviet Union on the basis of accepting the status quo. But before long another U.S. president, Jimmy Carter, launched the human rights campaign that melded with John Paul II's spiritual appeal and put the Soviet system on the ideological defensive. Carter also launched the technological renewal of the U.S. military. After the Russian invasion of Afghanistan, Carter became the first president in the entire Cold War to provide arms to an anti-Soviet resistance while also creating an infrastructure for a U.S. military presence in the Persian Gulf. Following Carter, Ronald Reagan articulated a more explicit challenge in all these domains to Soviet aspirations and pursued it with political determination and an effective popular appeal. The cumulative impact helped push Gorbachev's on-going perestroika into a general crisis of the Soviet system. Reagan's successor, George H. W. Bush, exploiting communism's denouement with diplomatic finesse, was the historical beneficiary.

Yet barely fifteen years after the wall came down, the once proud and globally admired America was widely viewed around the world with intense hostility, its legitimacy and credibility in tatters, its military bogged down in the new "Global Balkans" from Suez to Xinjiang (see Figure 4, p. 154), its formerly devoted allies distancing themselves, and worldwide public opinion polls documenting widespread hostility toward the United States. Why?

Confused Expectations

By 2006 it was difficult to recall the opportunity within America's grasp on the eve of the twenty-first century. The bloody twentieth-century contest for global domination—the most lethal conflict in history—had in effect just ended after two epic struggles. The capitulation of Nazi Germany and Imperial Japan, in May and August 1945 respectively, terminated the most brutal attempt ever to achieve global hegemony by direct force of arms. Almost half a century later the lowering of the red flag from the Kremlin tower in late December 1991 signaled not only the dissolution of the Soviet Union but also the final gasp of a perverse ideology that likewise sought global dominion.

May 1945 had already defined America's new standing as the world's premier democratic power; December 1991

1991

marked America's emergence as the world's first truly global power. Paradoxically, while the defeat of Nazi Germany elevated America's global status, America had not played a decisive role in the military defeat of Hitlerism. Credit in that regard has to go to the Stalinist Soviet Union, Hitler's odious rival. The American role in the political defeat of the Soviet Union, by contrast, was indeed central.

But the fall of the Soviet Union was neither as clear-cut nor as sudden as the earlier capitulation of Nazi Germany and Imperial Japan. It was messy, protracted, problematic in its implications, controversial in its causalities, and ambiguous in expression. Even the renaming of the Soviet Union as the Commonwealth of Independent States provoked questions. Was "Commonwealth" just a new name for the old Russian imperial system, or had the empire ruled for so long from the Kremlin truly fallen apart?

Contributing to the uncertainty was the fact that the discrediting of Soviet communism and the disintegration of the Soviet Union could not be ascribed to a single cause or even dated precisely. December 1991 was essentially a symbolic date, the culmination of a series of events, setbacks, errors, and actions from inside and outside the Soviet world that cumulatively swept away an increasingly rotten façade of dogmatically claimed invincibility and historical inevitability. Only later could the world fully appreciate the geopolitical and ideological meaning of this tectonic upheaval.

As a consequence, what seemed so very clear in 1945 was not at all clear in 1991. In 1945 the opportunity inherent in victory was naïvely defined as that of institutionalizing, in FDR's words, "a one world," even though that world was already dividing into two camps. Joy at the end of the carnage and hopes for universal peace had people literally dancing in the streets. Four and a half decades later, public reaction was more muted. In the great capitals of the victorious Atlantic alliance, there was no dancing in the streets when the Soviet Union dissolved. There were, to be sure, earlier outbursts of joy in the newly self-liberated Warsaw—and later in Prague and Budapest and the newly reunited Berlin—but the West expressed relief more than enthusiasm.

Complicating official perceptions and tempering public expectations at the end of the Cold War was the fact that the world America inherited as its ward on the eve of the twenty-first century was neither historically at ease nor truly at peace. Freed from the specter of a third global war between two superpower-led camps armed to the teeth with nuclear weapons, the world gave priority to narrower concerns. It was more susceptible to intensified nationalist passions and tribal hatreds, more tempted by the selfish luxury of indulgence in traditional antagonisms and religious violence. The end of the Cold War thus stirred not only hopes; it also ignited new passions, less universal in their ambitions but more primitive in their impulses.

Nonetheless, America's opportunity was in fact much greater than it had been in 1945, though less clear. American power faced no peer, no rival, no threat, neither on the western front nor the eastern front, nor on the southern fronts of the great Cold War that had been waged for decades on the massive Eurasian chessboard. Europe in 1991, though still semidivided, was busily "atlanticizing" itself. Its western portion was firmly tied to the United States through the NATO alliance, while its eastern portion, newly liberated from Soviet domination and redesignated as Central Europe, pined for admission to the privileged and rather idealized Euro-Atlantic community. Germany's reunification was just under way in an atmosphere of ecstatic emancipation as well as massive underestimation of the long-term social complexities and financial costs.

Moreover, the Atlantic alliance was about as strong as ever. In the final phases of the Cold War in 1989–1990, there had been disagreement over German reunification, with neither Margaret Thatcher nor François Mitterand (for historical reasons) sharing the determination of George H. W. Bush and Helmut Kohl to promptly end the country's partition. But the issue did not surface into public disagreement, and before long Germany's reunification was an accomplished fact. That a united Germany would effectively end Franco-German leadership of the emerging Europe (in which France had been able to piggyback on the partitioned Germany) was not yet apparent.

Even more promising was the overall state of American–European relations. The European Community was steadily deepening its unity, getting ready to adopt a common currency, and was poised to become the revamped and enlarged European Union in an atmosphere of transatlantic political cordiality. The notion of Atlantic partnership looked like a strategic reality, not only with regard to NATO (for which the Cold War victory was in itself a historic confirmation) but also applied to the relationship between the United States and the European Community beyond the geographic confines of Europe. There was talk of a more ambitious partnership that would provide a constructive sense of direction for a world now free of the potential horrors of World War III. America and Europe would thus jointly continue the West's traditional role of global stewardship.

That was the rhetoric of the time, the promise of the historic moment, the beckoning opportunity that a decade and a half later would appear both remote and unreal. The rise of Asia was still perceived as a distant prospect, and the leading Asian candidate for a major role was Japan, increasingly redefined as a "Western" democracy and a member of the trilateral club with America and Europe. Europe's progress toward greater unity was also breeding speculation regarding its future world role, with French geostrategists engaged in fertile projections of a restored Franco-European grandeur. Co-equality with America was not yet viewed as presaging a separation, and few envisaged today's Europe: more extensive in scope yet more distant from America while still impotent globally.

This hopeful new reality was hardly universal. The formerly imperial Soviet Union was experiencing pangs of nationalist separatism that promptly escalated into bitter ethnic violence. Multinational Yugoslavia disintegrated under the same pressures. Symptomatic of the times, this violence was pursued in the name of democracy and self-determination, both concepts associated with the victorious America and fervently proclaimed by the protagonists in the hope of eliciting U.S. sympathy and support. Former Soviet leaders were also busy reinventing themselves as the leaders of a national Russia or of other newly independent states. The most credible way for recent communist officials (notably in Armenia and Azerbaijan) to gain national popularity was to pursue territorial claims against some adjoining post-Soviet but similarly newly independent national entity.

Farther east, neither China nor Japan yet represented a serious challenge to America's sway or appeared poised to precipitate a regional crisis. But each was carefully reassessing the new global setting. China, still in the early stages of an impressively prudent, politically guided social transformation, was expanding the scope of private initiative from agriculture to small trade and manufacturing and then to larger-scale industrial activity, still with little awareness that within a decade and a half it would come to be perceived as potentially the world's next superpower. Its major national preoccupation was to prevent Taiwan's separation from gaining permanent international sanction. Geopolitically, China was still quietly savoring the success of its semicovert strategic collaboration with America in finally defeating the Soviet invasion of Afghanistan. The Sino-American relationship was malleable and, from the U.S. point of view, strategically productive.

Just next to China, barely touching the disintegrating Soviet Union's far eastern frontier, was the isolated North Korean regime. Suddenly bereft of Soviet protection and already deeply suspicious of the Sino-American strategic solidarity forged in response to the Soviet attack a decade earlier on Afghanistan, the North Korean dictatorship surreptitiously began to seek its own atomic weapons.

It is also easy to forget how very differently America saw Japan fifteen years ago. Throughout the second half of the 1980s, Japan was considered the rising superstate. The Japanese purchase of Rockefeller Center in New York City epitomized American fears that Japan might soon supplant America as the world's most vital and innovative economic power. Though that anxiety was not translated into policy, it helped stir the Japanese elite into a gradually intensifying awareness that Japan's place in the world could not be defined entirely by Article 9 of the U.S.-drafted Japanese constitution (which committed Japan to pacifism) or by the U.S.-Japanese defense treaty. That treaty, pledging America to Japan's defense, made Japan a de facto U.S. protectorate since it did not contain a reciprocal commitment like NATO's for Japan to come to America's defense. But in these respects the situation was likewise evolving, and Tokyo was increasingly recognized as part of a new trilateral partnership with the United States and the European Union.

The Soviet defeat in Afghanistan was followed by a deplorable American neglect of that country's future, a symptom of a wider indifference toward a region that, within a decade, became America's "Global Balkans": the huge area stretching from Suez to China's Xinjiang and rent by internal conflicts and foreign intrusion. Iran persisted in its fundamentalist hostility toward America and represented a potential regional problem, but its capacity to be a serious threat was sapped by an almost decade-long war precipitated by Iraq. Signs of opposition to religious extremism among Iran's intelligentsia and youth raised hope of an eventual evolution in more moderate directions.

The disappearance of the Soviet Union had the most immediate impact on Arab states, notably Iraq and Syria, that had relied on Soviet military and political support for their hostility toward Israel. Deprived of their strategic sponsor, the irreconcilable Arab states were now strategically adrift. The

wisdom of Anwar Sadat's earlier gamble on the American option (started with Nixon and consummated with Carter) now
seemed validated, and that lesson was not lost even on the
strategically misguided and tactically shortsighted Palestine
Liberation Organization. For the first time since Carter's
Camp David intervention of 1978, the prospect of peace in
the Middle East was not a mirage.

Finally, closer to home, Castro's Cuba was now a strategically isolated outpost. No longer the springboard for a conti-
nental revolution, no longer a demonstration of the Soviet
Union's global reach deep into the U.S. regional domain, no
longer even the base for more modest regional aspirations in
parts of Central America, the Cuban regime was now deprived of its key ally, its sponsor, its supplier of weaponry and
subsidies. Castro found China's fascination with the profit
motive in spurring economic growth to be ideologically suspect, while the dissolution of the Soviet Union seemed to
confirm his fears that liberalization was a highly contagious
infection that must be stamped out at the very outset. With
Castro's Cuba no longer representing the future of Latin
American politics, self-preservation dictated self-isolation.

The end of the Cold War also redefined global security.
With the likelihood of nuclear war between the two superpow-
ers rapidly receding, the issue of nuclear proliferation gained
new urgency, and an international consensus regarding how to
halt it came to seem more likely. At the time, neither North
Korea nor Iran was seen as the nuclear challenger that both
later became. But India's defiance of nonproliferation was
more than suspect, and its contagious impact on Pakistan was
self-evident. Israel's surreptitious acquisition was also hardly a

secret. South Africa's ongoing efforts were being closely scruti-
nized. The issue was clearly rising in significance.

The challenge of peacekeeping in states or regions incapable
of self-policing or subject to externally prompted disruptions
was another new complication. During the Cold War, any response to a civil war would inevitably have become an extension of the superpower conflict, and that had a dampening
effect on the issue itself. After the Cold War, collective peacekeeping was emerging as a legitimate and practicable regional
or international response. But endless questions were surfacing
regarding the obligations of the would-be peacekeepers, the division of authority, and the allocation of political leadership.

Last but certainly not least, the so-called Third World lost
its political role with the disappearance of the "Second
World." Often called also the Nonaligned Bloc, the Third
World's "nonalignment" no longer had any strategic meaning
following the disappearance of the Soviet Union. But its massive socioeconomic troubles were rising to the front of the
global agenda, largely driven by the growing impatience of its
vast and increasingly politically awakened populations. The
concomitant rise in the political importance of several key developing states—notably India, Brazil, and Nigeria—meant
that the central political, economic, financial, and social
dilemmas of the poorer portion of mankind would become an
increasingly important global issue.

The Search for Certitude

Immediately after the end of the Cold War, of course, it was
not clear what was in store. Was the revolutionary age ending?

Had the Cold War given way to eternal peace? Was the triumph of American democracy in its long struggle with Soviet totalitarianism the signal of democracy's universal relevance? Or were new threats appearing? What defining insight would illuminate the essence of the times and give purpose to America's new global status? Indeed, what should America's global role be?

In the immediate aftermath of America's emergence as the world's only superpower, these questions were not explicitly posed, at least not initially. America's coronation as global leader was a situational fact and not a global anointing. But the need for a policy-oriented interpretation of the new era was there, even if not yet felt on the public level, because of the cloudy complexity surrounding America's newly exalted perch on the top of the global totem pole. The answers could not come all at once.

Karl Marx once observed that consciousness usually lags behind reality. In other words, comprehension of sociopolitical change follows behind the change and does not precede or even accompany it. So it was with America's new historical dilemmas. There was a great need for coherent perspectives to replace the now obsolete premises that had guided American conduct on the world scene during the decades of the Cold War. Given the limited human capacity to comprehend complex reality and achieve a clear sense of direction, it took about a decade for these perspectives to gel and gain adherents.

At first, though only briefly, official discourse about the new global context and the opportunities it held was largely limited to a vague but positive-sounding slogan: "new world order." This had the advantage of implying many things to many people. To traditionalists, "order" suggested stability and continuity; to reformers the adjective "new" implied a rearrangement of priorities; to idealistic internationalists the emphasis on "world" conveyed the benign message that universality was now the lodestar of policy. But the administration promoting this slogan was voted out of office before its meaning could be fully spelled out, and the change to a new administration coincided with the surfacing of intellectually more refined and analytically more ambitious alternatives.

After this interlude of intellectual disarray, two increasingly irreconcilable versions of the past and visions of the future gradually emerged as the dominant American outlooks on global affairs. These should not be confused with ideologies as they came to be known during the twentieth century. They did not have a doctrinaire core or a formally proclaimed and allegedly infallible central text or little red book. Unlike their rigid totalitarian predecessors, they were mixtures of opinions, beliefs, slogans, and pet formulas. Each view expressed a predisposition and a framework for relatively flexible formulations based on a broadly shared, somewhat loosely defined set of convictions derived from history or social science or even religion. Their inclination toward dogmatism was tempered by the pragmatic traditions of American political life.

The first of these two world-organizing visions can best be described by the word most closely associated with its substance: globalization. The second is named for its doctrinal source: neoconservatism. Both ideas claimed to express the inner meaning of history. The first, which lacked the intellectual panache of its rival and was not as zealously propagated, emerged from several inspirations. Its advocates focused on the worldwide impact of technology, communications, and trade as well as financial flows, from which they drew fundamental lessons for America's position and role in the world. Two words best conveyed this vision's essence: interdependence and connectivity.

Globalization was catchy, trendy, and appealing worldwide. It implied progression or process as opposed to stasis, and also that this process was historically inevitable. Globalization thus conveniently fused objective determinism with subjective determination. The claim that interdependence was the new reality of international life in turn validated globalization as the legitimate policy for the new century. America's embrace of globalization implied innovation, historical momentum, and a constructive outreach, and it identified the American national interest with the global interest. Globalization was thus a convenient doctrine (and a fine source of slogans) for the victor in the just-ended Cold War.

While globalization suggested American leadership, America did not aggressively postulate it. But implicit in globalization was the notion of a central source, a point of origin, of inspiration and impulse—and America, though not named explicitly, was the only plausible candidate. Thus globalization bore no resemblance to the defunct communist doctrine, with its designated center of world revolution and infallible source of doctrinal truth in a world doomed to class struggle. Globalization merely hinted that America was inherently the source of energy and motivation for a worldwide process that was truly interactive and, in any case, fundamentally spontaneous. By embracing globalization, America would identify itself with a historical trend that was universal in scope, excluded no one, and set no limits on its potential benefits.

Here and there, of course, some groups would be displaced, a few narrow interests would suffer, and hurtful shifts in employment and production might occur. But to enthusiasts of the new era, these growing pains were a passing phase subject to almost automatic self-correction. Globalization would generate an ultimate equilibrium, with the redistribution of benefits for the many offsetting the initial hardships of the few. And America, as the spearhead of globalization, would find its global leadership both materially reinforced and morally legitimated.

Globalization benefited from another advantage: it was cheerfully optimistic. After the anxieties of the Cold War and the uncertainties of its initial aftermath, globalization was reassuringly sunny, optimistically asserting the benign effects of dynamic interdependence. Enthusiastically embraced by President Clinton, it conveyed a hopeful vision of an increasingly interdependent world progressing through multilateral cooperation "into the future." Its more fervent advocates even explained the fall of the Soviet Union as due less to the consequences of Stalinist crimes or the effects of anticommunist resistance, and more to the Soviet failure to respond promptly enough to the economic and technological requirements of the new age.

Last but not least, globalization had a ready-made and powerful constituency not only among America's business elite but also within the multinational corporate world that had grown rapidly during the waning decades of the Cold War. Indeed, much of this elite—anxious for direction and constancy in a world suddenly grown socioeconomically volatile—fervently hoped that the only remaining superpower would embrace the notion of globalization almost as a mantra.

Globalization did not become America's dominant worldview all at once. It gained momentum by accretion: by becoming a buzzword among the *cognoscenti* of world affairs, by being adopted in the myriad of international private and public institutions, and eventually by emerging as the favorite foreign policy concept of a historically upbeat American president. The case for multilateral cooperation henceforth was to be derived less from the fearful imperatives of international security and more from the beneficent promise of global interdependence.

Though initially embracing only an economic perspective, the advocates of globalization quickly realized that its appeal had to be fortified by a political component. An additional case for globalization then emerged: namely, that it would inevitably lead to greater democracy. Globalization thus gained a corollary proposition that became especially useful when the doctrine's critics began to charge that it was essentially a self-serving justification for the maximization of profits and that it was being used to rationalize investments in oppressive regimes that happened to be economically successful. The Tiananmen massacre in China in 1989 provoked severe criticism by human rights advocates that globalization enthusiasts were indifferent to human rights.

The intellectual lineage of globalization cannot be traced to specific and universally acclaimed intellectual classics, and certainly not to a single dogmatic source. It gained credence more through media propagation, sloganeering, newspaper op-eds, and international business conventions, and was popularized by books meant for general readership. The most notable of these was the *New York Times* journalist Thomas Friedman's *The Lexus and the Olive Tree: Understanding Globalization* (2000), which followed Benjamin Barber's popular *Jihad vs. McWorld: How the Planet Is Both Falling Apart and Coming Together and What This Means for Democracy* (1995). These were followed by the more academic works by Joseph Stiglitz, *Globalization and Its Discontents* (2002), and Jagdish Bhagwati, *In Defense of Globalization* (2004), as well as another highly popular essay by Thomas Friedman, *The World Is Flat* (2005). Globalization was thus simultaneously popularized and intellectually developed into almost a doctrine.

The rival doctrine, which came into flower under President George W. Bush, was starker in its demeanor, more pessimistic in its outlook, more Manichaean in its mood. In contrast to the economic determinism favored by the advocates of globalization ("Marxist" in that respect), neoconservatism was more militantly activist (and thus "Leninist"). In historical lineage, it deliberately harkened back to the Reagan phenomenon and legitimated itself by a retroactive and rather self-serving historical reinterpretation of that phenomenon, satirized at the beginning of this chapter.

Throughout his political career, Ronald Reagan had tapped into and benefited from the widespread popular feeling that America was floundering in the global contest with Soviet communism. By the mid-1970s Reagan was already seen by many Republicans as offering a more vigorous alternative to the historically pessimistic Nixon–Kissinger notions of détente. By the end of the decade, Reagan was the preferred

Republican choice for presidential candidate over the middle-of-the-road Gerald Ford. In 1980 Reagan defeated the sitting Democratic president, Jimmy Carter, who was viewed as not offering a clear-cut and sufficiently decisive counter to the Soviet challenge, and was associated with the humiliating seizure of American hostages in Tehran.

The coalition that took the lead in formulating the worldview for what came to be called the Reagan Doctrine (and to which neoconservative roots can be traced) was not predominantly Republican in origin. While Reagan electorally capitalized on the sense of unease among many conservative Republicans over the thrust of Nixon's and Kissinger's foreign policy as well as on the even more widespread Republican dismissal of Carter's record, the strategic content of the new Reagan Doctrine was heavily influenced by several Democrats with impeccable connections to President Truman or the vigorously anticommunist Senator Henry "Scoop" Jackson. Prominent foreign policy practitioners—including Paul Nitze and Eugene Rostow, who had served under several Democratic presidents, Richard Perle, who worked closely with Jackson, as well as policy theorists like Jeane Kirkpatrick—joined together in the late 1970s with a cluster of well-known conservatives to launch the Committee on the Present Danger. This committee propagated the call for a more muscular and doctrinally hard-hitting response to the Soviet Union.

The collapse of the Soviet Union a decade later provided the intellectual confirmation for a triumphalist view of America's role not only in the recent past but increasingly also in the future. The Soviet defeat was no longer to be seen as the outcome of a prolonged bipartisan effort but rather as a national salvation achieved by a charismatic leader guided by a cluster of true believers. This mythical revision of history compressed the entire Cold War into a single decade. Only under Reagan was the Soviet Union repelled and the cause of human rights embraced. Even John Paul II came to be portrayed as Reagan's personal recruit in a secret campaign to subvert the Soviet Union.

The verities drawn from this caricature of history were applied to the cloudy and complex realities facing America after its Cold War victory. To be successful, American foreign policy had to be derived from moral certitudes and pursued through a clear-cut good-versus-evil deciphering of the inevitably ambiguous historical imponderables. Public confusion was the luxury of the masses, compromise the failing of agnostics, and uncertainty an intellectual disqualification. Henceforth strength and clarity had to guide America, just as they had done when Reagan allegedly won the Cold War singlehandedly.

Translating these premises into a coherent, comprehensive doctrine took time. The new worldview emerged gradually, adapted to the new post–Cold War circumstances by the younger members of the original Committee on the Present Danger and by a cluster of energetic opinion shapers associated with conservative journals and think tanks. They shared the conviction that the challenge formerly posed by the Soviet Union and communism now emanated from the Arab states and militant Islam. Their strategic outlook on these issues was unabashedly sympathetic to the views of Israel's Likud party and gained significant support among American Christian fundamentalists. The latter provided a wider political base for the strategic views of the more elitist former.

Over a decade, a shared perspective, increasingly labeled as neoconservative, was thus systematized, expounded, and propagated in a series of books, articles, and jointly authored public manifestos addressed in some cases to the U.S. president or the Israeli prime minister. Increasingly dismissive of the postwar Atlantic alliance on the grounds that the Europeans were effete ("from Venus," unlike the muscular Americans "from Mars"), the new doctrine called for an assertive reliance on American political and military power. Though neoconservatism was articulated largely in short, often belligerent opinion pieces and articles, one of the early attempts at a more comprehensive formulation was a volume edited by Robert Kagan and William Kristol, *Present Dangers: Crisis and Opportunity in American Foreign and Defense Policy* (2000), an outgrowth of their 1996 article in *Foreign Affairs* entitled "Toward a Neo-Reaganite Foreign Policy."

Though propagated with the zeal typical of true believers, what came to be called the "neocon" doctrine did not contain a sweeping vision of the unfolding world in the aftermath of the Cold War. It was essentially an updated version of imperialism and was not primarily concerned with new global realities or novel social trends. Rather, it reflected specific neocon priorities in the Middle East. Amid the fear and anger aroused by the 9/11 attacks, the neocon option seized the moment and came into its own.

Without 9/11, the doctrine probably would have remained a fringe phenomenon, but that catastrophic event gave it the appearance of relevance. Before long, neoconservatives in the

Bush II administration translated its premises into official political and military doctrine. In the wake of 9/11 the doctrine also spilled over into domestic politics. The fear of terrorism, massively propagated, created a new political culture in which moral certainty began to verge on social intolerance, especially toward those whose ethnic origins or appearance could be viewed as giving grounds for suspicion. Vigilantism against immigrants or even wayward professors (especially with pro-Arab views about the Middle East) also reflected intensified self-righteous anxiety. Even civil rights came to be seen by some as an impediment to effective national security.

In the process of gaining wider social acceptance, this alternative worldview—advocated by the neocons as historically responsive to the new global circumstances—gained respectability from the unintended intellectual legacy of two genuinely insightful academic works. Their cumulative influence in shaping historical perceptions and piercing the post–Cold War fog provided a congenial intellectual context for a new vision. The earlier of the two was *The End of History and the Last Man* (1992) by Francis Fukuyama, who initially was associated with the neocon circles but later became the most cutting dismantler of the views of Charles Krauthammer, a leading neocon popularizer. The other, even more influential volume was *The Clash of Civilizations and the Remaking of World Order* (1996) by Samuel P. Huntington, who from the start had been a critic of the neocon prescriptions. Each book provided a sweeping interpretation of a unique moment in history, identifying its central essence and delineating its fundamental discontinuity.

Fukuyama's book, in the tradition of Hegelian and Marxist dialectics, brilliantly but somewhat misleadingly postulated that mankind's political evolution had crested with the victory of democracy. Initially much acclaimed, the argument was construed by many to mean that democracy was now the inevitable fate of mankind. (Neoconservatives seized on this interpretation after 9/11 as an activist prescription.) Perhaps only the title was misleading, given that the author later complained of having been misunderstood and claimed he had actually been making a less ambitious argument on behalf of evolutionary modernization. But his dramatic insight into the presumed historical inevitability of democracy provided a powerful case for those who advocated that America should propagate democracy, by whatever means available, as the central theme of U.S. policy in the Middle East. Dogmatic activism and historical determinism were thus conveniently wedded.

In a different fashion, neocons tapped Huntington's grand civilizational interpretation (in its sweep recalling Oswald Spengler's *The Decline of the West* and Arnold Toynbee's *A Study of History*, the first written shortly after World War I and the second after World War II) to validate their vision of an existential conflict with Islam over basic values. In that respect, Huntington's unintended political impact was even greater than Fukuyama's. Argued with great sophistication and with persuasively marshaled evidence, Huntington's case appeared to be a provocative prophecy that ought not be allowed to become self-fulfilling. Within a few years, however, and especially after 9/11, the "clash" became the widely accepted diagnosis of a global reality that as recently as 1990 had seemed truly remote.

The result was a Manichaean doctrine with which neither of the two scholars could ever have felt at home: democracy passionately propagated as the inevitable historical destination of a mankind engaged in an existential clash of basic values. But that is often the fate of great intellects; in his later years, George Kennan frequently complained that his pathbreaking and widely acclaimed treatise advocating containment of Stalinist Russia had been grossly distorted by those who lauded its analysis and sought to implement its prescriptions. In any case, the notion of a democratic "end of history" as the endpoint of a grand collision with fundamentalist Islam became for the neocons the clarifying beam of light piercing the post–Cold War mists.

These two visions—globalization as a rising tide and neo-conservatism as a call to action—came to dominate the political scene and overshadow alternative viewpoints. Still, the initially confused relief at the end of the Cold War gave rise to some notes of anxiety regarding the deeper condition of the West, especially in the moral and cultural realms. Questions were raised regarding the long-term viability of a Western culture that increasingly seemed to lack a moral compass. The absence of such a compass led me to wonder publicly (in a 1990 Georgetown University lecture entitled "Post-Victory Blues") whether the defeat of communism did in fact mean the victory of democracy.

Most immediately, that question focused on the future of the formerly communist nations of Eastern Europe and the failed Soviet Union. For Eastern Europe, the attraction of Europe served as a beacon and relevant example. The historic and geographic proximity of a unifying Europe could help overcome its forty-year subjection to communist doctrine. For Russia, the legacy of communism was twice as heavy and more deeply entrenched, and complicated by Russia's even older imperial traditions and lingering nostalgia for their revival. One would think that the logical course for the West, therefore, was to forge a long-term policy designed to draw Russia into a more binding relationship with Europe, but there is little evidence that anyone in Washington was giving this issue much constructive thought.

The gnawing philosophical uneasiness in the West, particularly in America, about the essence of dominant public beliefs thus made me concerned that neither of the two competing visions was historically sufficient for the challenge America now faced. This challenge was both strategic and philosophical. To what larger goal was the citizen of the democratic West, following communism's defeat, now committed? For many in the upper and middle classes, the answer was conveyed by two words: hedonistic relativism—no deeper convictions, no transcendental commitment, with the good life defined largely by the Dow Jones industrial average and the price of gasoline. If that was so, then the dichotomy between the hedonistic relativism of the West and the indigent absolutism of the suddenly impoverished inhabitants of the former Soviet space and the politically awakened developing world would only widen global divisions. The response had to come from a deeper moral definition of America's world role. Without this, America's global leadership would lack legitimacy.

A politically appealing moral impulse as a guide for policy ultimately has to be motivated by humanitarian concerns. It has to elevate human rights into a global priority. It has to respond to politically activated mass yearnings. An enlightened politics based on moral conviction should also stress consensual leadership and not Manichaean division. Conversely, the absence of moral conviction leaves opportunities for demagogy that exploits sudden crises and new fears. It was these concerns—more than doubts about the quality of personal leadership—that led me to write in *Out of Control* (1993) that "America's difficulty in exercising effective global authority. . . could produce a situation of intensifying global instability. . . and the reappearance of millennial demagogy," and even to speculate that "the phase of American preponderance may not last long, despite the absence of any self-evident replacement."

Ultimately the issue since 1990 has been the question: Does America have the stuff to lead the world at a time when the political and social expectations of mankind are no longer passive and the coexistence of varying religions and cultures is being compressed (as in a pressure cooker) by the impact of interactive communications? Three successive American presidents, George H. W. Bush, William J. Clinton, and George W. Bush, had the opportunity to answer that question, not as a philosophical abstraction but as a matter of real-life political choices. The first of these global leader/presidents sought to pursue a traditional policy in a nontraditional environment while America's two competing worldviews were still crystallizing. The second embraced a mythologized version of globalization in charge of mankind's destiny. The third pursued a militant commitment to prevail in a world dogmatically conceived as polarized between good and evil.

3

The Original Sin

(and the Pitfalls of Conventional Imagination)

Today we have entered an era when progress will be based on the interests of all of mankind. And awareness of this requires that world policy, too, should be determined by placing the values of all mankind first. . . . Further world progress is possible now only through the search for a consensus of all mankind, in movement towards a new world order.

MIKHAIL GORBACHEV, speech before the U.N. General Assembly,
December 7, 1988

A new partnership of nations has begun, and we stand today at a unique and extraordinary moment. . . Out of these troubled times. . . a new world order can emerge. . . in which the nations of the world, east and west, north and south, can prosper and live in harmony.

GEORGE H. W. BUSH, speech before a joint session of Congress,
September 11, 1990

THE "NEW WORLD ORDER" BECAME PRESIDENT
George H. W. Bush's trademark—the oft cited definition
of his world vision. But the phrase was neither his own nor an
accurate characterization of his foreign policy stewardship. In
a speech to Congress proclaiming his commitment to "a new
world order," Bush, not exactly giving credit where it was due,
confided that "this is the vision I shared with President Gorbachev" when the two had met weeks earlier. But Gorbachev
had used the phrase well before that. Bush I was not a visionary but a skilled practitioner of power politics and traditional
diplomacy in an untraditional age. Lacking a historical imagi-
nation, he appropriated Gorbachev's slogan but never seriously sought to implement it.

The Bush I presidency coincided with cascading upheavals
throughout Eurasia. Several crises were either ongoing or erupting throughout that vast continent, which over the previous four
decades had been the principal arena for the grand strategic
rivalry between the United States and the Soviet Union. That
rivalry involved confrontations along three strategic fronts: in
the west defined by NATO, in the east by the demarcation line
dividing Korea and by the Formosa Straits, and in the south, in
the Persian Gulf region, by the proclamation of the Carter Doctrine in reaction to the Soviet invasion of Afghanistan. These
fault lines were now being outflanked by rising political, ethnic,
and religious unrest in the Balkans, the Middle East, East Asia,
and especially within the Soviet bloc itself.

In responding to these continent-wide upheavals, Bush
showed both his strengths and limitations. He proved to be a

superb crisis manager but not a strategic visionary. He handled the collapse of the Soviet Union with aplomb and
mounted an international response to Saddam Hussein's aggression with impressive diplomatic skill and military resolve.
But he did not translate either triumph into an enduring historic success. America's unique political influence and moral
legitimacy were not strategically applied to either transform
Russia or pacify the Middle East.

In fairness to Bush, no U.S. president since the end of
World War II had to confront such intensive and extensive
global turmoil. Fortunately Bush was experienced and knowl-
edgeable and thus did not need a learning curve. He was well-
known to most foreign statesmen and generally respected. He
quickly fashioned his foreign policy team and took charge.
Whatever the subsequent reservations regarding his legacy, he
made good choices for his principal foreign counsellors. He
picked individuals who were close to him, followed his leadership, could work as a team, and accepted a basic division of
labor. The national security adviser, Brent Scowcroft, served
as the inside presidential counselor and friend of the Bush
family, while the secretary of state, James Baker, acted as the
reliable outside negotiator.

Bush clearly was the manager of U.S. foreign policy.
Strategic decisions flowed down from the top, not up from
the NSC staff or the State or Defense Departments. Bush
worked in close consultation primarily with three key top-
level advisers (the two mentioned above plus Secretary
of Defense Richard Cheney), all of whom he had known

personally for some time. But while consulting with them, and occasionally even bringing in outsiders for a one-on-one discussion in the Oval Office (I was invited to give advice on the Soviet Union and Poland), Bush was without question the primus inter pares and the final, well-informed, confident decision maker. The NSC system was smooth, focused, hierarchically clear, and responsive to a truly unprecedented set of historically major upheavals.

The world the Bush team faced was coming asunder, and a definable and historically comprehensible era was coming to an end. But the right course to pursue was not self-evident. Bush needed to define his priorities, look beyond just today and tomorrow, be clear about his sense of direction, and act accordingly. This he never quite did. He focused primarily on the delicate task of peacefully managing the dismantling of the Soviet empire and then on cutting Saddam Hussein's excessive ambitions down to size. He brilliantly achieved both but exploited neither.

The progressive fragmentation of the Soviet Union came to a head roughly at the midpoint of the Bush presidency, in December 1991. That date marks the onset of U.S. global supremacy. But the event was preceded and followed by mounting turmoil throughout the Soviet bloc. Any policy response to that turmoil was complicated by the violence and political upheavals erupting outside the Soviet sphere, in other parts of Eurasia. (The reader may wish to consult the basic chronology of the Bush term in the adjoining box to get a sense of the extraordinary pace of change confronting the Bush team during its four years in office.)

INTERNATIONAL CHRONOLOGY,
JANUARY 1989 TO DECEMBER 1991

February 1989. Just days after Bush takes office, Soviet troops withdraw from Afghanistan (which they had invaded at the end of 1979), having failed to crush persistent Afghan resistance backed by a semiovert coalition of the United States, Great Britain, Pakistan, China, Saudi Arabia, and others.

September 1989. Solidarity forms the first noncommunist government within the Soviet bloc. After being suppressed by the imposition of martial law in Poland in 1981, the Solidarity movement resurfaces like a phoenix in the late 1980s and in the summer of 1989 (less than half a year after Bush's inaugural) it forces the first free elections ever held in a communist-governed country. That unprecedented event precipitates a stampede throughout Eastern Europe, with Hungary emulating Poland in October, Czechoslovakia in November, and Bulgaria and Romania (the latter violently) in December.

June 4, 1989. The Tiananmen Square protest. In China, Deng Xiaoping's decade-long and increasingly dynamic program of socioeconomic reform unleashes a burst of productivity, innovation, and accelerated growth—as well as rising political ferment. Social unrest, especially among the younger intellectuals and university students, gives rise to a sudden outburst culminating in several days of demonstrations calling for democratization. The regime's bloody tank-led reaction in Tiananmen Square suppresses the most serious challenge to its rule since 1949.

November 9, 1989. The Berlin Wall comes down. The collapse of Soviet control over Poland, Hungary, and Czechoslovakia isolates the East German regime and prompts the dramatic dismantling of the Berlin Wall. In under a year Bush will override the concerns of principal West European allies and obtain reluctant Soviet acquiescence to the reunification of Germany in October 1990.

June 1989. Ayatollah Ruhollah Khomeini, the spiritual and political leader as well as the father of the fundamentalist regime in Iran, dies ten months after the end of an almost decade long and futile war between Iran and Iraq. Started by Iraq in September 1980, it became a prolonged and extraordinarily bloody war of attrition in which neither side could prevail. The conflict ground to an inconclusive end in August 1988, having caused close to a million fatalities.

August 1990. Saddam Hussein, presumably in an attempt to compensate for the costs of his Iranian misadventure, seizes Kuwait. In mid-January 1991, the United States begins an air campaign against Saddam's forces, followed in February by a ground offensive that crushes the Iraqi army and frees Kuwait.

1990. The crisis of the Soviet system gives the United States a free hand to cope with the Castroite and anti-American populist insurgency in Central America. The adventurist ruler of Panama, Manuel Noriega, has already discovered he has no allies. After the U.S. parachute assault on Panama City in December 1989, Noriega ended up in chains in an American prison. In 1990, both the left-wing insurgency in San Salvador and the Nicaraguan civil conflict come to an end, while the cutoff of Soviet economic aid to Cuba confronts the Castro regime with a severe economic crisis. In the fall of 1992, a month before the U.S. presidential elections, the North American Free Trade Agreement (NAFTA) is signed by the presidents of the United States and Mexico and the prime minister of Canada.

June 1991. In the Balkans, Croatia and Slovenia declare independence from Yugoslavia. A multiethnic state cobbled together in the wake of World War I, Yugoslavia has been suffering an internal crisis since the death of Marshal Tito in 1980. It now begins to emulate the fate of the Soviet Union. When Croatia and Slovenia, both increasingly resentful of Serbian domination, declare their independence, they set off a violent chain reaction that eventually destroys Yugoslavia altogether and several years later precipitates NATO action against Serbia.

1990–1991. Even before the final agony of the Soviet Union in December 1991, Lithuania, which was seized through Stalin's collusion with Hitler back in 1940, begins defiantly reclaiming its sovereignty. In early 1991 it is joined by Estonia and Latvia. Similar outbreaks of nationalist fervor take place in Soviet Azerbaijan and Georgia, each held by Russia for almost two centuries.

August 1991. An abortive coup by Soviet hard-liners against Gorbachev politically strengthens Yeltsin, who formally announces the disbanding of the Communist Party of the Soviet Union (CPSU). Three months later the Soviet Union itself is dissolved and Gorbachev is unemployed.

December 1, 1991. In a national referendum, the 50 million people of Soviet Ukraine vote for independence. During the second half of the 1980s, after three hundred years of Russian rule, Ukrainian agitation in favor of independence steadily intensified. In November 1990 Boris Yeltsin, the newly installed leader of Russia (but within the still existing USSR headed by Gorbachev), denounced Russia's imperial legacy in a historic speech delivered in Kiev. The referendum makes explicit the Ukrainian people's desire for complete independence.

Most of the events listed in the chronology were pregnant with complex international consequences, merited front-page headlines, called for careful assessments, and required difficult policy decisions. One or maybe two major international crises a year is not unusual for modern-day presidents, but for so many of them to occur almost concurrently was extraordinary. An entire era had suddenly come to an end. The collapse of the premier communist power and the cascade of revolutionary events that accompanied it swamped the policy-making process. In that context, the notion of a new world order provided at least some guidance and a convenient, even expedient framework. It was reassuring, hopeful, yet vague, and it provided room for a variety of policy responses.

Victorious Diplomacy

The most urgent task was handling the progressive fragmentation of the communist world in a manner that disabled it as a global challenge yet avoided a massive international upheaval. In their joint memoir, *A World Transformed,* Bush and Scowcroft candidly recall that they did not want a repetition in Eastern Europe of the turmoil of 1953, 1956, and 1968, in which initial liberalization produced a retrogressive Soviet reaction. The goal was transformation, not just accommodation.

A related concern of the Bush team was how to prevent Gorbachev from exploiting his unprecedented call for new forms of global cooperation to sow division within the Atlantic community. They worried that Gorbachev might even seduce France under François Mitterrand and Great Britain under Margaret Thatcher, both fearing a reunited Germany, into a deal that would buttress the cracking Soviet structure. The Bush team was aware that the European and American press was highly critical of the apparent lack of U.S. initiative in the face of Gorbachev's appealing overtures and the intensifying Soviet crisis.

Turmoil in the communist world was not confined to the Soviet realm. China too seemed on the brink of an explosion. While the Soviet-imposed regime was collapsing in Poland during the summer of 1989, social unrest also surfaced in China. With the boundaries between political control and socioeconomic liberalization blurring, an unprecedented outburst of massive student demands for democracy made it look for a moment as if the Chinese communist regime might implode as well.

The events of late May and early June 1989 that culminated in the student massacre on Beijing's Tiananmen Square provide an important clue to the strategy eventually pursued by the Bush administration toward the general crisis of communism. Setting up a statue named "the Goddess of Democracy," startlingly resembling the Statue of Liberty, in the very heart of the capital of the world's most populous communist state was an event pregnant with symbolic significance. Was the growing malaise of the Soviet system also erupting as a democratic revolution against the entrenched communist regime in China? Should the United States identify itself with that cause, placing at risk the strategically beneficial Sino-American cooperation initiated by the Nixon administration and much-deepened under Carter? What if the upheaval produced civil war in China?

Before these questions could be answered, the student rebellion was mercilessly crushed by tanks and lethal fire on June 4, the very day the communists lost power in Poland. The Chinese crackdown was brutal, decisive, and effective. (A year or so earlier, I had a one-on-one dinner in Beijing with Hu Yaobang, then the general secretary of the Chinese Communist party, and was amazed at the liberal reforms he professed to favor in an admittedly private meeting. His views indicated that at least a segment of the top leadership favored far-reaching changes in the political system. Not long after our meeting, Hu was removed from power, and he died shortly before the outbreak of the student unrest. But the top Chinese leadership was clearly divided even during the Tiananmen crisis.)

The seeming finality of the suppression made Bush's choice easier, and the U.S. response reflected the traditional mind-set of his administration. It involved caution, secret diplomacy, reassurance and continuity, while avoiding any ringing self-identification with the cause of the demonstrators. To be fair, the Chinese unrest, coinciding with the growing uncertainties in the Soviet bloc, posed a dilemma for

Bush. He did not want to jeopardize the strategic relationship that had developed between the United States and
China after President Carter's breakthrough in the normal-
ization of relations in late 1979, but he knew that the sympa-
thies of the American people and of Congress were with the
students.

Accordingly, he chose to react with a relatively mild public
rebuke, followed by a secret mission to Beijing by Scowcroft
to reassure the Chinese that the U.S. reaction would be per-
functory. Undertaken less than a month after the tragic events
in Tiananmen Square, the mission, quite remarkably, remained a secret. It may not have been quite as dramatic as
portrayed in the joint Bush–Scowcroft memoir, which
claimed that the Chinese almost shot down the national security adviser's plane by mistake. (Qian Qichen, the Chinese
foreign minister at the time, pointedly contests this assertion
in his memoir, *Ten Episodes in China's Diplomacy*.) The secret
visit did achieve its basic purpose: it conveyed to the Chinese
that American support for the democratic upheaval in Poland
did not apply to China.

That mission was followed a few months later, in early December, by a repeat trip by Scowcroft to Beijing, this time undertaken openly and involving a very public exchange of
goodwill toasts, which the American media (still unaware of
the earlier visit) roundly denounced as obsequious. Again,
Bush's purpose was to put a brake on any downward spiral in
relations, especially in view of American public outrage at the
continued repression of the Tiananmen activists. American
hopes for leniency were disappointed, but the administration
rationalized the Chinese intransigence as reflecting concern

over the almost simultaneous overthrow and execution of Romania's communist dictator, Nicolae Ceausescu.

According to Qian Qichen, shortly after Ceausescu's death the supreme Chinese leader, Deng Xiaoping, asked the visiting Egyptian president, Hosni Mubarak, to convey a message to Bush: "Do not get too excited over what happened in Eastern Europe, and do not treat China in the same manner." In retrospect, the two missions by Bush's closest aide must have appeared to the Chinese leaders as welcome and appreciated acts of deference but without much substance. To the Chinese liberalizers, even within the Communist party, they must have signaled U.S. indifference to their cause.

But China was not Eastern Europe, where events had a force and a dynamic all their own. They compelled far-reaching changes that neither Bush nor Gorbachev could control. After the stunning success of Poland's Solidarity in mid-1989, the division of Germany had become increasingly untenable. The progressive collapse of the communist regimes led to the fall of the Berlin Wall and placed German unification firmly on the agenda. For Gorbachev, the strategic task was to contain the fragmentation of the Soviet bloc lest it contaminate the still functioning Soviet system itself. He would ultimately fail to prevent this contamination, but until then Germany's future was a central concern. It was the main topic at the historic December 1989 encounter between Bush and Gorbachev, conducted on two warships near Malta. Held within just weeks of the dramatic dismantling of the Berlin Wall, the meeting began a thinly camouflaged capitulation by the Soviet leader regarding the centrally contentious stake of the Cold War in Europe: the future of Germany.

It was also Bush's finest hour. Not only was Soviet acquiescence to the political upheavals in Eastern Europe in effect
formalized, but a process of consultations was set in motion
that within a year led to the reunification of Germany, almost
entirely on Western terms. At a May 31 meeting in the White
House, Gorbachev explicitly accepted both Germany's unification and its continued membership in NATO. In return, he
was embraced with a series of well-meaning proposals em-
phasizing a constructive role for the Soviet Union in shaping a
cooperative global system to replace the Cold War divisions.
Financial assistance to the Soviet economy was also held out.
Implicit in all this was the notion that the new world order
would be based on collaboration among the major powers.
The Soviet Union was to be stripped of its external empire but
still treated as a preeminent global player.

It is impossible to overestimate the importance of the
peaceful reunification of Germany in October 1990 that followed this meeting. The fall of the Berlin Wall a year earlier
made reunification seem inevitable, but only if there was no
regressive Soviet reaction to the wall's removal. The Soviet
army was still in East Germany, and while the East German
regime was demoralized and confused by Gorbachev's apparent acquiescence, a change of mind in the Kremlin (or simply a change in the Kremlin) could have unleashed Soviet
forces. But the collapse of the Soviet-imposed and Soviet-
dominated regimes in Eastern Europe a few months earlier
made it much more difficult for the Kremlin to contemplate
a potentially bloody repression of German civilians, even if
limited to Berlin. East Germany had become an isolated
Soviet outpost.

It was the courage of the Solidarity movement in Poland—
and its contagious impact on the rest of Eastern Europe—
that produced the strategic isolation of the East German
regime. The Poles thus not only liberated themselves; by confronting Gorbachev with an impossible dilemma, they precipitated the reunification of Germany. For the Soviet leader, the
better part of valor was to negotiate an arrangement that
would help stabilize the situation while making the Soviet
Union a coequal partner with the United States in shaping a
"new world order." That at least was Gorbachev's strongly felt
personal inclination, which Bush skillfully exploited in Malta
and later in Washington.

Bush's performance deserves the highest praise. He ca-
joled, reassured, flattered, and subtly threatened his Soviet
counterpart. He had to seduce Gorbachev with visions of a
global partnership while encouraging his acquiescence to the
collapse of the Soviet empire in Europe. At the same time,
Bush had to reassure his British and French allies that a reunited Germany would not threaten their interests, even
while pressing the West German chancellor to recognize the
Oder-Neisse line (until then protected only by the Soviet
Union) as the western frontier of newly liberated Poland.

The reunification of Germany in late 1990 involved a mon-
umentally important shift in Europe's center of political gravity and thus also in the global geopolitical balance. Bush not
only persuaded Gorbachev to accede to unification but (with
West German Chancellor Helmut Kohl adding economic
sweeteners as an inducement) convinced him that a reunified
Germany of some 80 million people must be permitted to exercise freedom of choice in security and political matters.

That meant membership in both NATO and the European Community (soon to become the European Union). With Russia soon out of Germany and communism dismantled in Eastern Europe (soon redefined as Central Europe), most of the Soviet gains of World War II were lost.

Moreover, the reunited and newly self-confident Germany provided additional impetus for a new burst of European integration and, before long, also for NATO expansion. There could be little doubt that "Europe," now including a resurgent Germany with a strong American military presence, would soon move into the former Eastern Europe. The looming question was whether the process of accommodation to that new reality, which had been remarkably peaceful, would remain so given the rising turbulence within the Soviet Union. Compounding this uncertainty were the rising internal tensions in post–Tito Yugoslavia, like the Soviet Union a multinational state dominated by one ethnic entity.

It was in this context that "the new world order" became, for Bush, a quest for traditional stability. Forestalling the dismantling of either the Soviet Union or Yugoslavia became a priority that the Bush administration was loath to acknowledge publicly. Bush later disowned his efforts to preserve the Soviet Union in his own account of his presidency.

Having underestimated the potential for violence in Yugoslavia and overestimated the viability of the federal arrangements sustained only by the now deceased Marshal Tito, the Bush administration was caught unawares by the escalating Yugoslav crisis. Yugoslavia's failure to redefine the central government's powers caused a head-on collision between the dominant Serbian republic and two key components of the federation, Croatia and Slovenia. Their declarations of independence in June 1991 precipitated a prompt Serbian invasion, leading to a long and bloody war.

These developments intensified the Bush administration's fear that Gorbachev would lose control over the process of dismantling the Soviet bloc and that his perestroika might erupt into violence within the Soviet Union itself. Perhaps most important, Bush underestimated the genuine depth of non-Russian nationalisms within the faltering state and was seduced by the notion that the Soviet Union was synonymous with Russia.

(The idea that the Soviet Union had succeeded in shaping a Soviet national identity was particularly ingrained in the State Department bureaucracy. As a presidential assistant in the late 1970s, having long been convinced that the multinational character of the Russian empire was its Achilles' heel, I proposed a modest covert program designed to support the quest for independence by the non-Russian nations of the Soviet Union. In response, the State Department's leading expert on Soviet affairs persuaded the secretary of state that there was now in fact "a Soviet nation," a multiethnic mix much like America's, and that such an effort would be counterproductive. The program did go forward.)

The administration's misconceptions on this score were reflected in President Bush's infamous "Chicken Kiev" speech (given that merciless name by *New York Times* columnist William Safire), delivered in August 1991 in Ukraine's capital, with thousands of Ukrainians hoping to hear the president of the world's leading democracy endorse their aspirations to independence. To their bafflement, they heard instead that "freedom is not the same as independence. Americans will not support those who seek independence in order to replace a far-off tyranny with local despotism. They will not aid those who promote a suicidal nationalism based upon ethnic hatred."

This clumsily worded speech was widely interpreted as an attempt to preserve the Soviet Union by discouraging the Ukrainians from seeking independence. In self-defense, Bush and his national security adviser argued in their joint memoir that these remarks were not aimed at the Ukrainians at all but at Yugoslavia, as well as those parts of the Soviet Union where nationalist unrest was turning violent. They also asserted that the dominant point of view within the presidential team actually favored "the peaceful break-up of the Soviet Union."

But the record (notably the joint memoir) also reveals considerable concern in the Bush White House regarding the consequences of an eventual collapse of "a strong center" in Moscow, and thus a predisposition to help preserve it. James Baker, Bush's secretary of state, even urged that the United States "do what we can to strengthen the center." The lone dissenter flatly favoring the breakup of the Soviet Union was Secretary of Defense Cheney.

Despite these after-the-fact clarifications, in his speech to the Ukrainians Bush pointedly praised the ongoing reform in the Soviet Union, even trying to convince his skeptical listeners that it "holds forth the promise that Republics will combine greater autonomy with greater voluntary interaction—political, social, cultural, economic—rather than pursuing the hopeless cause of isolation." After endorsing the merits of "greater autonomy" (but not independence), Bush assured the perplexed

Ukrainians that America was looking forward "to doing business in the Soviet Union, including the Ukraine." In his conclusion, the president, referring to the audience as "Soviet citizens try[ing] to forge a new social compact," pledged that "we will join these reformers on the path to what we call—appropriately call—a new world order."

The speech provided unintentional insight into the strategy as well as the gut instinct guiding Bush's conduct. His status quo orientation, which by then lagged significantly behind events, led him to disregard the feelings of an audience that yearned for and expected sympathy but instead got a cold shoulder. The address, later disclaimers notwithstanding, in fact made a strong and explicit argument for the preservation of the Soviet Union and thus stood in opposition to Ukrainian aspirations for independence.

Fortunately it was not the last word and the administration did not remain wedded to it. Events beyond Bush's and Gorbachev's control soon made the speech irrelevant. Just days later, a failed coup against Gorbachev by Soviet hard-liners precipitated a stampede toward independence to which the United States could no longer remain indifferent. Ukraine proclaimed its independence and the administration had no choice but to acquiesce. The Soviet Union's death rattle came with the assertive and symbolically meaningful secession of the Baltic republics. With evident reluctance, Gorbachev finally accepted that reality in early September, and the United States, having previously warned Moscow that it could wait no longer, immediately extended recognition to the Baltic states.

In brief, political events raced far ahead of policy decisions. This disparity contributed to the uncertainty over where events were pointing, and policy makers increasingly found themselves playing catch-up. By the end of 1991, Gorbachev and the Soviet Union were history. Boris Yeltsin and a truncated Russia (with about 70 percent of the former USSR's territory and about 55 percent of its population) now had to be helped to recover from an upheaval that, with remarkably little violence, had all at once destroyed an ideology, an imperial system, an ambitious nuclear-armed global power, and a once vital totalitarian structure.

Not surprisingly, the Bush administration's top priorities were now to make certain the Soviet nuclear arsenal did not fall into unreliable hands in the successor states where they had been deployed, and to prevent "loose nukes for sale" from vanishing abroad. Thus a major focus of U.S. diplomacy during Bush's last year in office was the occasionally difficult negotiations with newly independent Ukraine, Belarus, and Kazakhstan over redeployment of these weapons to Russia itself. That issue demanded much time and effort, and the Bush team handled it with energy and skill, capitalizing on the enormously high prestige the United States enjoyed in the wake of the Soviet Union's demise.

Unfortunately the pace of events and the complexity of the tasks to be addressed in the dramatically changing U.S.–Soviet relationship over the preceding three years (not to mention the challenge posed in late 1990 by Saddam's seizure of Kuwait and the unprecedented U.S. military response early in 1991) left the Bush administration intellectually exhausted and creatively drained. Bush and his team successfully managed the dismantling of the Evil Empire, but they had had little time to plan the aftermath of a victory they (and others as well) had not fully anticipated. With little time left before the next presidential elections, the temptation to rest on one's laurels and rely on a vague slogan was too strong to resist.

The policy toward the new Russia was therefore rich in rhetoric, generous in gestures, and strategically vacuous. Boris Yeltsin was hailed as a great democratic leader, partly to compensate for the cold shoulder Bush gave him during his rise to power so as not to offend Gorbachev. But not much thought was given to developing a comprehensive program for political and socioeconomic transformation that would firmly link Russia to Europe. Monetary aid did flow to Russia, but in a mindless way, without a guiding conception and unconnected to a disciplined program of economic and financial reform (of the sort that, for example, Finance Minister Leszek Balcerowicz was able to impose in Poland). The financial assistance to the Yeltsin government was not trivial. By early 1992 over $3 billion had been sent for food and medical grants, over $8 billion for balance-of-payments support, and close to $49 billion for export and other credits and guarantees. Much of this was simply stolen.

While Yeltsin was being hailed and Russia's chaotic government embraced by America and Europe as a fellow democracy, Russian society was plunging into unprecedented poverty. By 1992 economic conditions were comparable to those of the Great Depression. Making matters worse was the presence of a swarm of Western, largely American, economic "consultants" who too often conspired with Russian "reformers" in rapid self-enrichment while "privatizing" Russian industrial and especially energy assets. Chaos and corruption made a mockery of official Russian and American pronouncements of Russia's "new democracy." The legacy of corruption came to haunt Russian democracy long after Bush's watch had ended.

More perplexing was the uncertain status of the Russian state, an issue that demanded but did not receive sensitive attention. The dissolution of the Soviet Union in December 1991 was initially meant to be followed by a new formation called the Commonwealth of Independent States (CIS). The tight union dominated by the Kremlin was to be reformed into a loose confederation still coordinated from Moscow. But that concept was aborted by the national aspirations of the non-Russian states, for whom the end of the Soviet Union meant national sovereignty and nothing less. Foremost among these was Ukraine, and its determination to be independent defined the CIS as a moribund fiction.

The Bush administration did not know that by 1992 it had little time left to address these new issues within a comprehensive strategic perspective. Justifiably proud of their skillful performance in managing the dismantling of the Soviet empire but surprised by that empire's rapid fragmentation, and with less than a year left before the next presidential election, the Bush team let the new challenges of post–Soviet Russia run their course for the time being, to be dealt with in a second term that never arrived. The new world order was rhetorically redefined to include Yeltsin's Russia, but without any new substance and without a longer-range response to the post–Soviet world.

Similarly, having been misled by top officials who believed that Yugoslavia would endure without Tito and then suddenly confronted with hostilities among the constituent republics, the Bush team simply let the Yugoslav crisis drift. It is quite revealing that the Bush–Scowcroft memoir, which in over 590 pages describes in great detail the major challenges the authors faced, contains just four brief references to Yugoslavia, some not even a full sentence long. With the United States indifferent and Europe impotent to do anything on its own, the Yugoslav crisis grew unchecked, becoming both bloody and terminal. One has to assume that Bush would have focused on it in a second term, but as it happened, the festering and increasingly violent conflict was bequeathed to his successor as unfinished business.

The administration's stance toward Afghanistan was equally passive. When the Soviet army withdrew in February 1989 after a nearly decade-long war of unprecedented brutality, the country was devastated and its economy ruined, with nearly 20 percent of its population living as refugees in nearby Pakistan and Iran, and with no effective central government. The Soviet-installed regime in Kabul was overthrown within months by the anti-Soviet resistance, which then splintered into violently conflicting factions. The United States, which had provided support for the resistance under Presidents Carter, Reagan, and Bush, made little effort to galvanize the international community to help Afghanistan stabilize politically and recover economically. The consequences of that neglect were felt later, long after Bush had left office.

Nonetheless, Bush's handling of Gorbachev, whose belated efforts to reform the ailing Soviet Union set in motion the crisis that Bush then exploited, was a historic accomplishment of far-reaching consequence, especially when one contemplates what might have happened if the American president had been less skillful or lucky. There could have been bloody Soviet repression in Eastern Europe, massive violence in the Soviet Union, or even some unintended East–West collision. Instead, the subsequent peaceful emergence of a democratic Europe, tied to NATO and embraced by the nascent European Union, tipped the historic balance in favor of the West.

Forsaken Triumph

By the fall of 1990, the Bush team's intense preoccupation with the crisis in the Soviet bloc had to compete with another time-consuming and attention-demanding claimant on the presidential agenda. It is awe-inspiring to consider that in the midst of the extraordinarily complex effort to peacefully dismantle the Soviet empire, the Bush administration simultaneously had to face a sudden security threat in the Persian Gulf and mount a major diplomatic and military response to the Iraqi seizure of Kuwait. The challenge there, as in the Soviet case, was not only how to respond to an immediate dilemma but—just as important—how to devise an enduring solution for a conflict-torn region.

Paradoxically, the coincidence of these two major crises gave Bush greater latitude in coping with the second. The reader should bear in mind the chronology of unfolding events (see also page 50): the Iraqi invasion of Kuwait took place in August 1990, while Gorbachev was still maneuvering for a face-saving way to acquiesce to Western terms for German unification. Compounding his difficulties was the internal crisis set in motion by the collapse of the Soviet satellite regimes in Eastern Europe less than a year earlier and now escalating into a threat to the Soviet Union's very survival. By late 1990 the Soviet empire no longer existed, and the tottering Soviet Union was just a year away from dissolution. Russia desperately needed Western economic aid; the Soviet leader was a mere shadow of his former self, and America ruled the roost. The U.S. president could act without worrying that the Soviet Union might stand in his way.

Saddam Hussein must have calculated otherwise. Perhaps he figured that he was striking at a time when both the United States and the Soviet Union were absorbed with other matters. He probably also felt that he could still rely on the Soviet presence on the U.N. Security Council to veto any coercive response by the United States. For the preceding three decades, the Soviet Union had been increasingly active politically and militarily in the Middle East. It lost some ground in Egypt, especially after the Carter–Sadat collaboration of the late 1970s, but Iraq and Syria remained beneficiaries of Soviet weapons largesse, and Iraq's military establishment and tactics were heavily influenced by Soviet military advisers. It seemed reasonable to expect that the Soviet Union would still provide international cover for Iraq's regional ambitions.

Saddam must have also concluded that the United States, not only busy in Eastern Europe but with Vietnam fresh in its memory, would not be inclined to react forcefully. He may have also been misled by a conversation with the U.S. ambassador, who seemed to signal a lack of U.S. interest when Saddam hinted at his intention to invade Kuwait. But he could not have been more wrong. His fatal error was to misunderstand the new geopolitical realities. After the events of 1989 and 1990, Bush stood tall as the world's first-ever global leader, and the United States was almost universally acknowledged as the world's only superpower.

In that setting, Saddam's action was not only a challenge to the traditional U.S. position in the Persian Gulf (especially to America's oil interests in Saudi Arabia and the United Arab Emirates) but—perhaps even more important—to America's new dominance in the world and Bush's new global status. Whatever the legitimacy of Iraq's historic claims to Kuwait, the invasion was an act of defiance. Bush felt that America had to respond, though he wisely realized that the response had to respect international law and the interests of other countries.

Bush learned of the Iraqi invasion early in the morning of August 1, 1990. By his own admission, his preoccupation with the Soviet crisis had prevented him from paying much attention to the Persian Gulf. But he and his principal advisers promptly concluded that the United States had to lead an international response legitimated by collective U.N. condemnation, reinforced by sanctions, and backed by a contingent military buildup. International circumstances favored this strategy. The Soviet Union, in no position to argue, joined the United States in condemning the Iraqi move on August 3. A few days later, the king of Saudi Arabia, fearful that the Iraqis would sweep south, took the unprecedented step (given Saudi religious sensitivities) of accepting a defensive U.S. troop deployment on Saudi territory. Not long afterward, the Arab League also resolved to send Arab forces to defend Saudi Arabia.

From the start, the British strongly supported Bush's efforts to induce a prompt Iraqi withdrawal, and the United States was also backed by the French. Margaret Thatcher, the British prime minister, still triumphant over her victorious confrontation with Argentina over the Falkland Islands, was especially firm in urging decisive action. Bush also called in a favor from the Chinese, who were reminded of his forbearance in reaction to the Tiananmen Square massacre. With a 13 to 0 vote in the U.N. Security Council demanding Iraq's withdrawal, Iraq's international isolation and condemnation were accomplished barely two weeks after the invasion.

But international solidarity did not resolve the question of whether force would have to be used, and if so when. Bush himself, according to his memoirs, had concluded by mid-August that force would be necessary, even though some of his National Security Council advisers urged that sanctions be given more time. Gorbachev took the same position, his earlier alacrity in condemning the Iraqi aggression notwithstanding. The Chinese foreign minister recalls in his memoirs that China also urged patience before any recourse to armed force.

Bush spent the next several months pursuing a three-pronged agenda. First, he worked on implementing the sanctions. Second, he continued diplomatic maneuvers to evade the occasionally public and more often private efforts, especially by the Russians, to find Saddam some face-saving formula for withdrawal from Kuwait. Third, he oversaw the buildup in Saudi Arabia of a large expeditionary U.S. military offensive capability, reinforced by British, French, and the politically important Arab contingents. U.S. troop presence in Saudi Arabia by the end of the year grew to 500,000.

The diplomatic effort to isolate and stigmatize Saddam was as critical to success as the military buildup. By the end of

FIGURE 2 ❖
MILITARY PARTICIPATION IN PERSIAN GULF WAR OPERATIONS

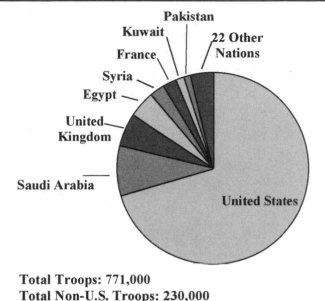

Total Troops: 771,000
Total Non-U.S. Troops: 230,000

Prepared by Brett Edkins

1990, solid international support, including a tough Security Council resolution, helped ensure congressional authorization for the contingent use of force in the event of Iraqi noncompliance. Despite last-minute Soviet efforts to mediate a settlement, a massive and very destructive air campaign against Iraqi forces commenced on the night of January 15–16, followed on the night of February 23–24 by a ground campaign undertaken largely by U.S. forces. For symbolic reasons, Arab forces were designated to enter Kuwait City, and the Iraqi forces capitulated on February 27. 1991

At this point the historical appraisal of what did and did not happen becomes complex and speculative. One could argue that Bush's response to Saddam's aggression against Kuwait produced both his greatest military victory and his most inconclusive political outcome. The decision to go to war in early 1991, to have people die, to compel by force a desired outcome, was ultimately a crucial test of Bush's character and leadership. But the geostrategic consequences of this personal triumph turned out to be more problematic. Saddam was defeated and humiliated but was not left powerless. The region's malaise continued to fester.

Bush himself recalls being surprised to learn that Saddam still had more than twenty divisions at his disposal, including the Republican Guard (his elite units). He also professes to have been "disappointed" that Saddam stayed in power, but that does not tell us much about what efforts—if any—were exerted to ensure a different outcome. In any case, the issue of Saddam's continued hold on power nagged at the Americans, and there is a tragic connection between what did not occur in the winter of 1991 and what did occur in the spring of 2003. Had the outcome of the first Gulf War been different, a subsequent U.S. president might not have gone to war in Iraq.

What we do know is that the prompt cease-fire in February 1991 left Saddam with sufficient military force to crush the Shiite rebellion that sprang from his military defeat, a rebellion that may have been stimulated by U.S. calls for popular action. The resulting resentments fed into the intense Sunni–Shiite hostility that so vastly complicated the political scene in Iraq years later, after Saddam's fall. They also furthered the Arab image of a United States toying with Arab aspirations in order to maintain its hold over the region's oil.

Might Bush have pursued a political trade-off—exile for Saddam Hussein in exchange for the nondestruction of Iraqi armed forces? Bush and his team have argued that ousting Saddam would have required storming Baghdad, and that redefining their goal in midinvasion could have split the coalition and alienated its Arab participants. But a determined attempt to turn the shocked and demoralized Iraqi military leadership against Saddam might have worked. The Iraqi forces were in chaotic retreat by the time of the cease-fire. An ultimatum to Saddam Hussein—step down and go into exile or your forces will be wiped out as they flee—reinforced by a publicly or covertly conveyed guarantee to the Iraqi military leaders (and even to some Baath party leaders) that they would be allowed to share in power might have transformed the military triumph into a political success.

The desert victory in Iraq thus was not exploited strategically, either in Iraq or in the region as a whole. The close and very visible Anglo–American cooperation in dealing with Saddam's challenge, personified by the Bush–Thatcher duet, gave rise to a pervasive view in the Middle East of America as the eager inheritor of the British imperial mantle and acting largely under British instigation. Most Americans remain blissfully unaware of the old Arab grievances against British imperial domination, the unfulfilled promises of emancipation from Ottoman rule, and the periodically brutal repression of rising Arab nationalism. In the eyes of many conspiracy-prone Arabs, America was acting under Downing

Street's influence and picking up where the British imperialists had left off.

This was particularly regrettable given Bush's success in enlisting Arab states in the campaign against Saddam Hussein. That coalition created an opportunity for America to use its extraordinary standing to tackle head-on the region's most bitter conflict, the cause of much suffering and a major source of rising anti-American feeling, namely, the Israeli–Palestinian conflict. As Dennis Ross, the principal Middle East negotiator for President Clinton and known to be a staunch friend of Israel, has noted, "No issue evokes more anger or a deeper sense of injustice throughout the Middle East than the Israeli-Palestinian conflict."

Bush initially seemed prepared to undertake a comprehensive initiative to end that conflict. Even before the 1991 war, he had signaled his intention to do so despite a Likud government in Israel that was committed to the expansion of Israeli settlements in the Palestinian territories. Back in May 1989, four months after the inaugural, Bush's secretary of state bluntly told AIPAC, the primary Israeli–American lobby, "For Israel, now is the time to lay aside, once and for all, the unrealistic vision of a greater Israel. . . . Forswear annexation. Stop settlement activity. . . . Reach out to Palestinians as neighbors who deserve political rights." In March 1990 Bush himself declared, "My position is that the foreign policy of the United States says we do not believe there should be new settlements in the West Bank or in East Jerusalem."

But the attention of the White House was soon diverted to Saddam's occupation of Kuwait. During the military conflict that followed in early 1991, Bush's major concern regarding

Israel was to keep it from retaliating for Saddam's deliberately provocative rocket attacks on Tel Aviv. Bush feared that an Israeli counterstrike would cause the Arab participants to defect from the anti-Saddam coalition. In return for their forbearance, the Israelis were granted $650 million in emergency aid, beyond their $3 billion annual military aid package.

On March 6, 1991, shortly after the cease-fire, Bush issued a public statement announcing his intention to seek a comprehensive peace between Israel and its neighbors. At the same time, he reiterated the long-standing U.S. position that peace must be based on U.N. Resolutions 242 and 338 (a formula strongly opposed by Israeli Prime Minister Shamir) and must provide both "for Israel's security and recognition, and at the same time for legitimate Palestinian rights." Notably, there was no mention yet of a Palestinian state.

In mid-1991, Shamir demanded a $10 billion loan guarantee while refusing to halt the construction of settlements. With Shamir having already budgeted the required funds for 1992, pro-Israel lobbyists mounted a full-court press for congressional approval. By confronting the issue head-on, Bush not only obtained congressional approval for a 120-day freeze on pertinent legislation but also imposed an embargo on a loan guarantee for Israel, which lasted until Shamir lost the 1992 elections and was replaced by Yitzhak Rabin of the Labor Party. Rabin acceded to Bush's demand for a halt in settlement construction, and the embargo was lifted one month before Bush lost his own election.

Thus, for a while it seemed as if the United States would use its leverage to jolt all the regional parties into a final, long-delayed accommodation. By the fall of 1991, Bush had already enlisted Gorbachev (who, however, would be out of power two months later) to issue a joint U.S.–Soviet invitation to the conflicting parties—Israel, Syria, Jordan, Lebanon, and the PLO—to attend a peace conference scheduled to start on October 30 in Madrid. That conference set in motion a protracted process of multilateral and bilateral negotiations, with the United States monitoring and cajoling, and Moscow essentially observing. This ultimately led to the creation of the Palestinian Authority and Arafat's return to the West Bank, but only after Shamir was replaced by Rabin. Nevertheless, the peace process bogged down during 1992 in contentious squabbles without a fundamental breakthrough.

Between Saddam's military defeat in February 1991 and Bush's political defeat in November 1992, the United States chose not to present the Israelis and the Palestinians with an explicit U.S. formula for comprehensive accommodation beyond Bush's general statement of March 1991. While a negotiating process between the parties did ensue, it could not overcome the extremely different notions of what an eventual accommodation ought to entail. On their own, the Israelis and the Palestinians could not bridge their most hostile suspicions of each other.

As a consequence, despite high expectations and a major investment of effort by the Bush administration, the Madrid peace conference's eventual accomplishment was the PLO's recognition of Israel's right to exist, in return for which the PLO was permitted to establish a subordinate administration under continued Israeli occupation in the West Bank and Gaza. The "comprehensive peace" Bush had spoken of remained as elusive as ever.

We will never know if a more ambitious and explicit definition of the central quid pro quos of the peace accord, publicly and firmly articulated by the U.S. president, would have produced the desired agreement. It would not have been easy for either side to defy an American leadership that enjoyed unprecedented prestige following the collapse of the Soviet Union and the defeat of Iraq. America was admired and, most importantly, seen as endowed with historical legitimacy. Had that prestige and legitimacy been exercised to depose Saddam and then to press hard for a Middle Eastern peace accord, the region might have looked very different a decade later. Perhaps Bush calculated that it would not be wise to push hard during a presidential election year, and he might have intended to do so after his re-election. In 1991 he had every reason to expect that he would return to office, but by mid-1992, with his political ratings on the slide, he was widely perceived as neglecting domestic affairs.

To sum up, in 1991 and early 1992 Bush had more leverage to accomplish a breakthrough to peace than any U.S. president since Eisenhower. But he never tried to use his extraordinary standing in the region to press the parties to adopt explicit principles regarding the key contentious issues, nor did he commit America to such principles through a binding and public declaration. That was the moment to put on record a U.S. commitment to several fundamentals: no right of return for the Palestinians, no significant Israeli expansion beyond the 1967 lines, territorial compensation for any changes, a formula for sharing Jerusalem, and demilitarization of the eventual Palestinian state.

The unfortunate result was that Bush's unconsummated success in Iraq became the original sin of his legacy: the inconclusive but increasingly resented and self-damaging American involvement in the Middle East. In the dozen years that followed, the United States came to be perceived in the region, rightly or wrongly, not only as wearing the British imperialist mantle but as acting increasingly on behalf of Israel, professing peace but engaging in delaying tactics that facilitated the expansion of the settlements.

The deployment of U.S. troops on the sacred ground of Saudi Arabia provided the stimulus for religious fanatics to articulate a doctrine of hate for America. The Sunni Wahabis echoed, in a somewhat different terminology, the Iranian Shiite leadership's earlier labeling of America as the "Great Satan," and a fatwa by a hitherto obscure Saudi militant (from a wealthy Saudi family) targeted America as the desecrator of holy Islamic sites and the principal sponsor of Israel. Al Qaeda thus made its appearance on the world stage.

A second term might have given Bush the time to become a truly innovative president, the shaper of a new historical era. Certainly, his record in handling the agony of the Soviet empire deserves the highest plaudits, and it is doubtful that his predecessor, Ronald Reagan, would have performed as skillfully. But in the Middle East, a stunning military victory was diminished into a mere tactical success whose strategic legacy gradually became negative. The unfinished business of both the Israeli–Arab conflict and the Iraqi cease-fire came to haunt Bush's successors. Arabs increasingly saw America's role in the region not as an innovative influence but as a replay of the colonial past.

Bush's legacy suffered from a further shortcoming. Not only did he leave behind an unexploited opportunity in the Middle East and no strategy for the consolidation of democracy in Russia, but he was slow in responding to mounting evidence that existing restraints on nuclear weapons proliferation were beginning to crack. Would-be proliferators appear to have drawn a pernicious conclusion from the Gulf War: to deter the United States or one's own neighbors, an atomic bomb is a priceless asset. Understandably preoccupied with the Soviet bloc and then Iraq, the Bush administration did not mount a serious effort, either on its own or by mobilizing international consensus, to nip in the bud the increasingly visible efforts by India and Pakistan, and the still ambiguous activities of North Korea, to acquire nuclear weapons.

Late in 1989 a U.N. resolution cosponsored by Pakistan and Bangladesh in favor of a South Asia nuclear-free zone was passed by a large majority, but it failed in practice because India opposed it. The following April the Indian prime minister in effect signaled India's intention to go nuclear by asserting that India had "no choice but to accept and worthily rebuff" the allegedly growing Pakistani challenge. The United States then terminated most of its economic and military assistance to Pakistan, but that action did not inhibit India's efforts. The Indians and Pakistanis engaged in brief public relations maneuvers designed to put the onus for the race on the other. By 1992, Bush's last year in office, both governments were acknowledging that they were seeking a nuclear weapons capability—though, of course, only to offset the other.

Anxiety also began to surface that North Korea might also be seeking nuclear weapons. To persuade the North Korean regime to accept international supervision, the United States removed its nuclear weapons from South Korea in late 1991 while the South Korean government issued the Declaration on the Denuclearization of the Korean Peninsula, which included a pledge of self-denial. These steps were taken to satisfy the North Korean regime's demands for reassurance and to obtain its acceptance of International Atomic Energy Agency inspections. In response, North Korea ratified in 1992 the safeguards agreement with the IAEA, some six years after signing the nonproliferation treaty. It also became compliant by admitting to the IAEA that it had been reprocessing small amounts of uranium and possessed some plutonium, submitting its own report on its nuclear program and accepting initial IAEA inspections of its facilities.

The Bush administration, by now heavily preoccupied with its reelection campaign, was not predisposed to apply America's monopoly of power and prestige to muster a major international effort, and even less to undertake one on its own to bridle the nuclear weapons aspirations of North Korea, India, and Pakistan (with Iran quietly drawing appropriate lessons). Moreover, the lack of a priority concern with nonproliferation became especially apparent when the administration's draft Defense Planning Guidance was leaked to the press in late winter 1992.

This document addressed the new realities inherent in America's novel status as the sole global superpower. It contained sensible and tough-minded recommendations for exploiting the new circumstances created by the fall of the Soviet Union and the defeat of Iraq. The zone of U.S. predominance was to expand eastward in Europe and be firmly con-

THE ORIGINAL SIN   81

solidated in the Middle East. The document postulated a view heavily influenced by traditional balance-of-power politics while bluntly asserting American global military superiority.

The latter preoccupation may have contributed to the administration's curious indifference to nuclear proliferation, which reflected the absence of a broader, more ambitious sense of direction for a world that at that moment generally welcomed U.S. leadership. American military superiority by itself could not provide needed answers to a perplexed world on the cusp of a widespread political awakening, to an Asia stirring, a Europe uncertain of its mission, or a Russia beset by confusion. After a public outcry over the March draft report, the final version, officially released in May, attempted to take adverse foreign reactions into account by tempering its imperious overtones.

Nonetheless, the document planted the intellectual seeds for the policy of unilateralist preemption and prevention that emerged a decade later. By then the authors of the working draft, who were midlevel officials in 1992, had reappeared as senior Defense Department and NSC officials, while its principal sponsor, Secretary of Defense Cheney, resurfaced in 2001 as the vice president of the United States. In 1992, however, lip service had to be paid to the notions of a new world order, and thus the final document offered reassuring assertions of the U.S. commitment to existing alliances and enhanced cooperation with states previously viewed as adversaries.

These modifications notwithstanding, the defining characteristic of the document, stated more explicitly in the draft but reflected still in the final version, was an emphasis on

America's power and its commitment to a traditional world-view. The authors made much of the fact that the distribution of power had changed with the disappearance of the Soviet Union. But the new or emerging dimensions of global politics, as well as the opportunity to infuse new meaning into the existing international institutions long overshadowed by the Cold War, were ignored. With the end of the Cold War, the world was yearning for something more ambitious, more dramatic, more visionary. Power alone could no longer contain the awakened aspirations of peoples who knew in detail what they did not like, but whose desires were much vaguer, conflicted, and vulnerable to manipulation by false prophets.

In brief, George H. W. Bush's greatest shortcoming was not in what he did but in what he did not do. He left office enjoying unprecedented global respect. He earned it. But as a global leader he did not seize the opportunity to shape the future or leave behind a compelling sense of direction. The historical moment called for a grand vision for the world at large and for decisive U.S. political intervention in the Middle East. It called for a burst of global architectural innovation like the one that followed World War II, in keeping with the new opportunities for international cooperation involving Russia, China, and other emerging powers. None was forthcoming, and not much was foreshadowed should Bush have won a second term.

Robert Browning wrote, "A man's reach should exceed his grasp, or what's a Heaven for." By 1992 a remarkably successful diplomat and determined warrior had turned his promising call for a new world order into a reassertion of the more familiar old imperial order.

4

The Impotence of
Good Intentions

(and the Price of Self-Indulgence)

There is no longer division between what is foreign and what is domestic—the world economy, the world environment, the world AIDS crisis, the world arms race—they affect us all. January 21, 1993

At the dawn of the 21st century a free people must now choose to shape the forces of the Information Age and the global society. January 20, 1997

Today we must embrace the inexorable logic of globalization. February 26, 1999

Globalization is not something we can hold off or turn off. It is the economic equivalent of a force of nature—like wind and water. November 17, 2000

The train of globalization cannot be reversed. December 8, 2000

UNLIKE HIS PREDECESSOR, PRESIDENT BILL CLIN-
ton had a global vision. The historical determinism inherent in the concept of globalization fit perfectly with
Clinton's profound conviction that America, to justify calling
itself "the world's indispensable nation," must also renew itself. For Clinton, foreign policy was thus largely an extension
of domestic politics. Years later, he recalled being struck during the 1992 election campaign by President Bush's apparent
lack of interest in domestic affairs. The entire country saw
Bush glancing impatiently at his watch during one of the
presidential debates. Domestic issues seemed to bore him.
That insight helped shape Clinton's electoral strategy, and his
presidency.

Domestic renewal thus became the central theme of the
first Clinton term. But since foreign affairs could not be ignored, Clinton's emphasis on globalization provided a convenient formula for melding the domestic and the foreign into a
single, seemingly coherent theme while freeing him of the obligation to define and pursue a disciplined foreign policy strategy. Globalization thus became the theme that Clinton
preached with apostolic conviction both at home and abroad.
During a November 2000 visit to Vietnam he called globalization "the economic equivalent of a force of nature"; a few
months earlier he had told the Russian Duma that the world's
"defining feature is globalization."

The relative downgrading of international affairs in Clinton's priorities is reflected revealingly (though probably unintentionally) by the striking contrast between George H. W.
Bush's memoir and Clinton's. Bush's 566-page volume (written with his national security adviser) is devoted—with some

justifiable pride in the authors' accomplishments—exclusively to foreign affairs. Even Bush's distinguished wartime military service is not memorialized. Clinton chose instead to write a lengthy account (1,008 pages!) of his life—discreet in its treatment of some personal issues—in which his eight years' management of foreign affairs as history's Global Leader II is summarized rather superficially in about 15 percent of the total. Even Clinton's secretary of state during his second term, much more activist and assertive than her predecessor, devoted a relatively large part of her memoir to personal recollections not related directly to foreign policy strategy and implementation.

Paraphrasing Clausewitz's famous dictum that "war is a continuation of politics by other means," one might say that Clinton (in contrast to Bush) viewed foreign affairs as a continuation of domestic politics by other means. This view also influenced the way foreign policy decisions were made under Clinton and how his principal foreign policy appointees were selected. Clinton's first appointments for national security adviser (Anthony Lake), secretary of state (Warren Christopher), and secretary of defense (Les Aspin) conveyed a dual message: his team was strongly liberal in outlook, concerned with humanitarian issues, sensitive to domestic politics, and not inclined to personal, bureaucratic, or military assertiveness. Lake was especially concerned with the growing humanitarian crisis in Africa. Christopher, much older than Clinton, was respected for his self-effacing caution and passive demeanor (a common joke in Washington was that "he is so lifelike"). Aspin was a professional domestic politician with a quick and searching intellect but no experience in strategizing or in large-scale organizational management. Neither collectively nor individually were they likely to press a demanding agenda of foreign policy involvement on the new president.

The second term, somewhat belatedly, saw some adjustments. The president by then had become drawn into a more intense engagement, and his foreign policy team projected a higher level of activism. Sandy Berger, the second-term national security adviser, was a politically savvy pal of Clinton's and thus more confidently assertive. The new secretary of state, Madeleine Albright, was strongly committed to the expansion of NATO and infused a more sharply defined sense of geopolitical direction into NSC deliberations, with emphasis on Europe. That focus subsequently proved to be an important asset when the Yugoslav crisis exploded into large-scale violence. Bill Perry, Clinton's second secretary of defense, appointed early in the first term, was a respected defense specialist. In the second term he gave way to Bill Cohen, a former Republican senator who infused a degree of bipartisanship into defense and national security issues.

More striking still was the difference in the modus operandi from the Bush era. Bush's management style in foreign affairs was top-down, confined to a narrow circle of personally known senior decision makers, with the president firmly in command and the national security adviser his discreet alter ego. Clinton's style could not have been more different. It violated most rules of orderly process and defied easy characterization. Foreign policy deliberations in the Clinton White House were more like a "kaffeklatsch" than any usual notion of high-level policy making. They involved pro-longed meetings with no strict agenda, rarely beginning or ending when scheduled, and featured spontaneous participa-tion from a variety of White House officials. Some of the par-ticipants were involved primarily in domestic affairs and attended the NSC deliberations on their own volition, inter-vening at will in foreign policy deliberations. The president, especially in the first term, was more a participant than the dominant voice, and when a meeting finally ended, it was of-ten unclear what if any decisions had been reached. This made life difficult for the national security adviser because it was not always evident what actions needed subsequent in-teragency implementation and coordination.

Colin Powell, Clinton's chairman of the Joint Chiefs, put it succinctly to David Rothkopf in Rothkopf's comprehensive study of the NSC system, *Running the World:* "Now [if] you had come in from Mars and didn't know who was who, you would have joined that conversation [not knowing] who the president was." Powell described the atmosphere as if "we were now at the coffeehouse." Though things settled down over time and became somewhat more orderly, other senior officials nonetheless recall that even during Clinton's second term there was no one dominant voice regarding foreign pol-icy. Neither the president, his vice president, the national se-curity adviser, nor the secretary of state took charge. Personal influence was fluid and the resulting bureaucratic disarray was never entirely overcome.

The newly established National Economic Council (NEC), by contrast, functioned in a more disciplined and professional manner, perhaps because foreign policy seems to be an area in which almost anyone feels entitled to air opinions, while economics and finance are more esoteric. There was a dominant cabinet-level official clearly in charge, and this made the difference when the Clinton administration was confronted by financial crises in Mexico and in Southeast Asia.

The priority placed on domestic affairs and the view of foreign policy as an extension of domestic politics had a significant side effect: Congress, increasingly pressed by foreign policy lobbies with external connections, was encouraged to broaden its attempts to legislate foreign policy. This was not an entirely novel phenomenon. In the past, especially when foreign policy was being shaped on a bipartisan basis, the executive branch occasionally contrived with Congress to produce legislation furthering U.S. foreign policy goals and strengthening the negotiating hand of the executive branch by seeming to limit its options. In the post–Vietnam War era, the emphasis shifted to legislation that was actually designed to impose on the executive branch specific goals favored by particular foreign policy lobbies, or simply to limit the executive's freedom of action. This tendency became marked in the 1990s and has continued into the present, with a series of legislative acts passed due to energetic promotion by well-endowed lobbies committed to advancing the particular foreign policy interest of this or that ethnic community, irrespective of the views of the White House or the State Department. The most active and successful of these have been the Israeli–American and the Cuban–American lobbies, both of which have the resources to make a difference in congressional fund-raising and command large electoral support in two major states, New York and Florida.

Further complicating the foreign policy-making process, though also partially in reaction to Clinton's one-dimensional, optimistic view of the world, the Congress, the mass media, and interested lobbies have periodically embarked on propaganda campaigns to expose what might be called America's "enemy of the year." Press campaigns followed by hostile congressional resolutions and speeches have focused, for example, on Libya, then Iraq, then Iran, then China, each time stressing the danger each successive country allegedly posed to the United States. The paradox of an objectively secure and mighty America, victorious in the Cold War, searching for global demons to justify its subjective insecurity created fertile soil for the fears that became so pervasive after 9/11.

The problem Clinton faced and indirectly contributed to, but never quite resolved, was that the post–Cold War world was not quite as benign as his cheerfully deterministic notions of globalization implied. But in fairness to Clinton, the highly volatile state of the world made it difficult to define clear foreign policy priorities and identify the principal geopolitical threats. Unlike Bush I, President Clinton did not confront challenges with the enormous potential for good or evil inherent in the terminal crisis of the Soviet bloc and Soviet Union, or in the defiant act of aggression posed by Saddam's invasion of Kuwait.

Instead, Clinton confronted a flock of disparate and occasionally overlapping international problems, some peaceful and some violent, that reflected the increasingly restless and simmering global conditions that surfaced in the wake of the highly polarizing American–Soviet Cold War. Two contrasts with the earlier Bush presidency thus stand out. In addition to the appearance of a multiplicity of complex crises in the absence of truly grand challenges, the chronology below signals a more constructive emphasis in U.S. foreign policy on emerging global issues outside the traditional realm of power politics.

INTERNATIONAL CHRONOLOGY, JANUARY 1993 TO DECEMBER 2000

1993. The North Korean nuclear challenge surfaces in the wake of IAEA allegations of cheating. The United States begins the long process of deliberation regarding the scope of NATO while the Maastricht Treaty sets the stage for the transformation of the European Community into the European Union. An attempt is made to blow up the World Trade Center in New York City. Violence breaks out in Bosnia. After a bloody showdown, U.S. peacekeepers are withdrawn from Mogadishu in Somalia. The Oslo Accords seem to signal a breakthrough in Israeli–Palestinian relations.

1994. NAFTA goes into effect following an energetic legislative effort by Clinton. In February NATO initiates its first offensive action in Bosnia. Russia is included informally in the G7, the annual summit of major industrial democracies. China is granted most favored nation trade status by the United States. The North Korean nuclear proliferation issue heats up but then in October results in the U.S. and North Korean Agreed Framework for mutual concessions. In September Clinton seeks to reassure Russia on NATO expansion. In the same month the U.S. dispatches peacekeepers to Haiti, while genocide in Rwanda gains momentum unimpeded. Late in the year Russia attacks Chechnya.

1995. The WTO is established. Iran surfaces as a companion problem to that posed by North Korea with the signing of the agreement for Russian construction of the Bushehr nuclear plant. Prime Minister Rabin is assassinated in Israel. The first of two confrontations with the People's Republic of China occurs in the Taiwan Straits. Informal consensus develops within the Clinton administration in favor of NATO expansion to the east. Russia strongly protests the NATO air campaign in Bosnia, but the military intervention leads to the Dayton Agreement in November, terminating Bosnian hostilities.

1996. The U.S. signs the Comprehensive Test Ban Treaty. The first formal bilateral U.S.-North Korean talks take place. The second confrontation in the Taiwan Straits results in a peaceful standoff while the U.S. and Japan upgrade their alliance. The Taliban seizes Kabul. Clinton publicly reveals, just prior to congressional elections, an unspecified intention to enlarge NATO.

1997. Former Chinese premier Deng Xiaoping dies. Hong Kong reverts to China. NATO-Russia Founding Act is signed in May. Six weeks later Poland, the Czech Republic, and Hungary are formally invited to join NATO. Pakistan announces nuclear capability. Asian financial crisis breaks out. Kyoto Protocol on reduction of carbon emissions is drafted, but U.S. Senate votes its reservations by 95 to 0.

1998. Russia formally joins the G8. U.S. conducts punitive bombing in Iraq. Both India and Pakistan conduct nuclear bomb tests. Wye River talks sponsored by U.S. between Israel and Palestinians make little progress. Al Qaeda attacks U.S. embassies in East Africa. U.S. retaliates by bombing Afghanistan and Sudan. Japan and PRC issue a joint declaration of reconciliation. U.S. signs Kyoto Protocol but it is not submitted for Senate ratification.

1999. NATO undertakes a campaign to evict Serbia from Kosovo. NATO is formally expanded. International force, with U.S. participation, restores peace in East Timor. U.S. Senate rejects Comprehensive Test Ban Treaty. Second Chechen war breaks out with Russian offensive. Yeltsin resigns as Russia's president. International agitation against globalization rises. Dow Jones exceeds 10,000. Y2K scare spreads in the United States.

2000. Vladimir Putin is elected president of Russia. Second intifada breaks out. President Assad of Syria dies. Al Qaeda bombs the USS *Cole*. U.S. secretary of state visits North Korea and the deputy to Kim Jong Il visits Washington. U.S. stock market begins sharp decline. Long delayed Camp David II talks, scheduled before U.S. presidential elections, end in failure. At the end of December Clinton signs the Rome Statute of the International Criminal Court but indicates that he has no intention of submitting it for Senate approval.

Shaping the Future

Clinton's youth, intelligence, and eloquence, as well as his articulate idealism, made him the perfect symbol of a benign but all-powerful America, the world's accepted leader. He offered what Bush could not or did not have the time to offer: an appealing vision of the future. Articulated within Clinton's rosy view of a history driven by "the inexorable logic of globalization," the arms race would give way to arms control and nonproliferation, wars to peacekeeping and nation building, and national rivalries to institutionalized global cooperation subject to supranational rules of conduct.

Even if Clinton overemphasized and mythologized the benign effects of globalization, he did, to his credit, recognize the new global opportunity facing America. By giving it eloquent rhetorical recognition—which helped legitimate America's new superpower status in international public opinion—Clinton projected an appealing image of a young leader sensitive to the technological and ecological dilemmas confronting humanity, aware of the moral deficiencies of the global status quo, and ready to mobilize mankind in a common effort to cope with problems no longer susceptible to resolution by individual nations.

The disappearance of the Soviet Union, with its commitment to global ideological uniformity, created three significant opportunities for Clinton to pursue his agenda of enhanced global security and cooperation:

❖ First, it made possible more comprehensive American and Russian initiatives to limit the arms race between the two nations that for so many years had drained social capital while intensifying international tensions. The less antagonistic relationship permitted more effective limitations on the testing, production, and proliferation of nuclear weapons.

❖ Second, the disappearance of the bipolar world created the possibility for an even wider global system of shared security. The system would start with more effective impediments to the proliferation of nuclear weapons among an increasing number of states.

❖ Third, the end of the division of Europe meant that a larger, viable Europe linked closely to America through the Atlantic community could now emerge. That wealthy, democratic community could then serve as the politically and economically energizing inner core of responsible global cooperation.

The Clinton administration pursued all three objectives, though with mixed results. Some goals proved to be too ambitious, with rhetoric far exceeding capability. The pursuit of others collided with entrenched legacies of the past, which surfaced when the Cold War disappeared. Some suffered from the president's declining capacity to inspire and lead because of his personal difficulties and because of America's unwillingness to overcome its self-gratifying social habits and accept some of the limits on national sovereignty that it expected from others.

The collapse of the Soviet superpower and the Russian economic implosion created especially propitious circumstances for the pursuit of the first goal, halting the arms race between the United States and Russia. At first there was real progress. The Nunn–Lugar program financed the consolidation of the Soviet nuclear arsenals within purely Russian territory. Started in Bush's last year and completed in 1996, it avoided the instant emergence of Ukraine, Belarus, and Kazakhstan as nuclear powers. It is hard to imagine what the security of Europe would have looked like a decade later with these three nations as nuclear powers.

The 1993 START II agreement with Russia also provided for significant cuts in American and Russian nuclear arsenals and signaled another major step toward halting the arms race that had lasted almost forty years. Within a year, it was followed by the Mutual Detargeting Treaty, further reducing any lingering fears of a destructive nuclear exchange. Steps were also taken to enhance the security of Russian depots for the storage of warheads and other nuclear materials. Moreover, thousands of nuclear weapons and delivery systems were deactivated or dismantled. The United States also obtained a Ukrainian commitment to the Nonproliferation Treaty as a nonmember state in return for enhanced economic assistance.

Ukraine was also persuaded to abandon its contract concluded in the waning days of the Soviet Union, to construct a nuclear plant in Bushehr, Iran. However, the United States subsequently did not live up to its promise to compensate the Ukrainian plant in Kharkhiv, which had to give up construction of the Iranian plant. The issue became more complicated in early 1995, when Russia made an arrangement with Iran to complete the partially built facility.

The cumulative effect of these steps was to transform an insecurity-breeding race for strategic supremacy into a more predictable standoff. Each side retained the capacity to inflict horrendous damage on the other. Both remained free to improve the effectiveness of their now numerically limited arsenals. Both could even calculate that they might gain a significant strategic edge through the technological enhancement of their weapons or perhaps some new capability to disrupt the other's command-and-control arrangements. But for the time being, both America and Russia were relieved of the dread that an open-ended, uncontrolled arms race could suddenly confront one of them with the choice to either capitulate to an overwhelmingly more powerful opponent or face largely one-sided destruction.

The end of the political challenge posed by the Soviet Union was thus followed in the mid-1990s by the termination of the most threatening and potentially destructive arms race in human history. While the end of the Cold War did not produce wider international disarmament, the successful imposition of a rational cap on the most expensive and politically volatile rivalry nonetheless provided the world a reassuring confirmation that the Cold War was truly over.

For Clinton, the cap on the arms race also signified a subtle revision of Bush's doctrine of strategic supremacy. It codified America's de facto promise to Russia that the United States would not exploit its advantage in wealth and technological know-how to obtain the decisive strategic superiority that each side had once feared the other might somehow attain. At the same time, given the overall superiority of the American economy—magnified by the simultaneous implosion of the Russian economy—the United States could devote its resources to improving its ability to rapidly project conventional military forces around the world and enhancing their capabilities. America thus could gain a free hand worldwide that Russia could not even attempt to match. In brief, both America and Russia gained in security, but America also gained uncontested global military reach.

Though the entire world significantly benefited from this strategic bargain between the two states having the capacity to unleash a monstrous holocaust on a few minutes' notice, there was also growing international recognition of the need for a wider and more effective system of security. The ominously mushrooming prospect that relatively impoverished countries might acquire nuclear weapons for use in political conflicts with their immediate neighbors warranted a new form of containment. As noted in the previous chapter, this danger was emerging during the Bush presidency from North Korea, India, Pakistan, Libya, and perhaps Iran as well. Only an energetic response from an America no longer tied down by the Cold War could stand in the way.

The challenge posed by North Korea broke into the open only a couple of weeks after Clinton's first inauguration. The International Atomic Energy Agency (IAEA), unconvinced by North Korea's submission regarding its nuclear program, responded with a demand for special inspections. The North Korean regime not only refused but bluntly announced that it intended to withdraw from the Nonproliferation Treaty (NPT), citing Article 10 of the treaty, which allows withdrawal for national security reasons. This act of open defiance confronted the new American world leader with his first crisis—one with implications reaching far beyond North Korea.

One can only speculate about North Korean motives, but several considerations pertinent to America's exercise of world leadership are germane here. North Korea cannot have failed to notice the swift, one-sided American military victory in the 1991 Gulf War against an opponent with no credible deterrent to America's overwhelming conventional capability. Moreover, the collapse of the Soviet Union and the ensuing American–Russian strategic accommodation probably made North Korea anxious that the role of the Russian nuclear forces had been reduced to deterring unilateral American nuclear intimidation only of Russia itself. The Russian nuclear umbrella no longer extended over the remaining communist states. The Chinese, meanwhile, had been quite deliberately maintaining a posture of minimum strategic deterrence, sufficient from their point of view to deter any U.S. threat to China but not wide-ranging enough to protect its militant and unpredictable neighbor. Lacking nuclear protection the North Koreans presumably concluded that their interests would be best served by the surreptitious acquisition of a national nuclear capability sufficient to inflict significant damage on vital U.S. interests, even if initially only within South Korea or Japan.

The cat-and-mouse game that followed is not a record of which the Clinton administration had much reason to be proud. The United States responded to North Korea's abandonment of the NPT with a reasonable proposal to help North Korea pursue a peaceful nuclear program. North Korean graphite nuclear reactors, capable of generating components for atomic weapons, would be replaced with light-water reactors. Additionally, the United States would pledge not to use force against North Korea. This constructive proposal, however, was not balanced by any credible punitive threat— for example, a naval blockade of North Korean shipping—at a time of maximum U.S. freedom of action and almost complete North Korean isolation. By late 1993, the CIA estimated that North Korea had already separated about twelve kilos of plutonium, enough for one or two weapons.

The next several years saw periodic North Korean gestures of accommodation, followed by defiance. In 1994 North Korea agreed to allow inspections, then refused them, then announced its withdrawal from the IAEA, then concluded "an agreed framework" with the United States providing for the termination of the North Korean weapons program in exchange for U.S. and South Korean economic inducements and promises of normalized economic and diplomatic relations. Over the next several years, the United States and North Korea also engaged in fruitless debates over the North Korean missile programs, including the export of North Korean missile technology. At one point in 1996, the Clinton administration toyed with the idea of a preemptive strike at North Korean nuclear facilities, but decided to impose limited economic sanctions instead. That was followed by wider regional consultations regarding the North Korean problem, first with Japan and South Korea and later with China.

The inconclusive character of these initiatives prompted South Korea to open up a direct channel to North Korea, the so-called Sunshine Policy. This initiative both reflected and stimulated a rise in pan-Korean nationalism among the South Koreans and growing discomfort with the country's status as an American protectorate. China was the principal geopolitical beneficiary, quietly exploiting these sentiments—as well as Korean antagonism toward Japan—to enhance its regional influence.

In 1999 a former Clinton defense secretary visited the North Korean capital to explore informally the possibility of a wide-ranging North Korean–U.S. accommodation. In late 2000, just two weeks before the U.S. presidential elections, Clinton's secretary of state, Madeleine Albright, also called on the North Korean leader in an effort to achieve a breakthrough in relations. As a sweetener, she even raised the possibility of a visit by President Clinton to the dictator in

Pyongyang, thereby conveying to her hosts more propitiation than persuasion.

We may draw three inferences from this record. First, at no point was North Korea credibly confronted with the prospect that the cost of its determination to acquire nuclear weapons might outweigh the benefit of acquiring them. Second, U.S. hesitations made it possible for Pyongyang to exploit South Korea's growing desire for reconciliation with the North, thereby undercutting an effective joint U.S.-–South Korea negotiating posture. Third and most important, throughout the process North Korea was able to continue seeking nuclear weapons, with the result that by 2001 U.S. officials concluded that it had surreptitiously produced several. North Korean defiance in effect prevailed.

American opposition to the Indian and Pakistani quests for nuclear weapons showed a similar pattern of futility, though here, admittedly, America enjoyed even less leverage. As the North Korean saga was unfolding, the United States intensified its efforts to obtain an indefinite extension of the NPT, which the Clinton administration considered the bedrock of its nonproliferation efforts. This initiative produced considerable resentment among countries that felt America was trying to institutionalize a permanent global inequality in national security. The critics of U.S. efforts noted that the move to renew the NPT indefinitely was not being matched by any significant efforts to reduce the number of states with nuclear weapons or to facilitate greater equality in atomic energy programs.

Two related developments compounded the Clinton administration's difficulties. First, the French government conducted a series of nuclear tests in the Pacific, arguing that they were necessary for the continued credibility of what it called the "European" deterrent but which in fact was obviously a French national deterrent. Though by 1995 the United States succeeded in getting the NPT indefinitely renewed, the French nonetheless proceeded with the tests in defiance of self-serving Pakistani and Indian protests. China conducted its own underground tests soon after.

The French tests in turn undercut political support in Congress for the Clinton administration's efforts to ratify the Comprehensive Test Ban Treaty (CTBT), which the administration viewed as an essential component of an internationally approved firewall against the spread of nuclear weapons capability. Following an acrimonious and increasingly partisan debate, the U.S. Senate unexpectedly defeated the bill to ratify the treaty, strengthening the view of many abroad that the American quest for nonproliferation was driven by essentially monopolistic motives.

In this context, both India and Pakistan felt free to acquire their own nuclear arsenals. As early as 1993, the U.S. administration realized that its policy of one-sided sanctions against Pakistan was not effective. By leaving India free to pursue its programs, the sanctions created irresistible pressure on the Pakistani government to respond in kind; at the same time, sanctions solely targeting Pakistan were hurting other American interests in the region (notably American–Pakistani cooperation in dealing with the postwar turmoil in Afghanistan).

Thus by 1997 two additional nuclear powers were poised to step forward despite persistent but obviously floundering U.S. efforts to prevent them. That fall, the Pakistani prime minister publicly declared that "Pakistan's nuclear capability is now an established fact." Early the next year, Pakistan test-fired a long-range missile capable of carrying a nuclear warhead (which then led to the reimposition of U.S. sanctions on Pakistan). In May, India responded by conducting five nuclear tests, one of them clearly of a thermonuclear weapon. Two weeks later, Pakistan answered with six underground nuclear explosions. At that point, the United States, Japan, and some other nations registered their determination to impose more severe sanctions, but it was too late; two new members had forced their way into the hitherto exclusive five-member nuclear club.

The open success of India and Pakistan, and the covert success of North Korea, doubtless had a contagious effect on Iran. During the 1990s, largely under congressional pressure abetted by the Israeli lobby, the United States adopted a series of legislative acts with their edge pointing sharply at Iran that had the effect of inhibiting any serious American–Iranian dialogue. The Iran Foreign Oil Sanctions Act of 1995, imposing additional oil and trade sanctions, quickly followed by the highly restrictive Iran-Libya Sanctions Act, made it virtually impossible for the Clinton administration to respond to the occasional (though ambiguous) Iranian gestures toward a more constructive dialogue with the United States. Whether such a dialogue would have inhibited Iranian nuclear efforts is impossible to judge, though it is reasonable to assume that the Iranians were impressed by the success of their neighbors to the east. In any case, it became increasingly evident that Iran's nuclear program, started many years earlier under the shah (with some early French and perhaps even Israeli assistance), would be a major bone of contention in American–Iranian relations.

The failure to contain nuclear proliferation in the Far East and in South Asia conveyed a sobering lesson. Short of a unilateral military action—with all its unpredictable consequences—even the world's only superpower could not by itself dissuade a country firmly determined to acquire nuclear weapons. A successful preventive effort would have required an early concentration of attention on the issue, determined and coordinated mobilization of other concerned states, and the early formulation of a program including both incentives for self-restraint and costly consequences for continued pursuit of nuclear weapons. In the early, heady days of American unilateral supremacy, it was easy to ignore incipient proliferation in the belief that an intimidating response by the United States would eventually suffice to halt it. The lesson bequeathed to the Clinton administration's successor was that even given the great asymmetry of power between the United States and any would-be proliferator, the only alternative to war was genuine international cooperation, mounted on at least a regional basis, at an early stage of the nuclear challenge.

The third opportunity for constructive enhancement of global security and cooperation in the wake of the Cold War occurred in Europe. The end of the division of Europe meant that the American–European partnership could now be upgraded and acquire even greater global significance. Exploiting this opportunity involved increased Europe-wide economic and political integration, as well as the mobilization of the combined influence of the Atlantic community to address common global problems.

The sudden end of the division of Europe drew attention to the craving of the newly liberated postcommunist states to become integral and above all secure parts of the Atlantic community. Clinton's response to this dilemma took several years to evolve, but in the end it became the most constructive and enduring part of his foreign policy legacy. The overlapping realities of the NATO alliance embracing twenty-seven members (twenty-five of them European) and a twenty-five-member European Union meant that the old slogan of "a transatlantic partnership" could at last acquire real substance. That partnership had the potential to inject political vitality into a sustained effort to shape a more cooperative world system.

The catalytic issue for the alliance's renewal was the question of NATO expansion. At first this seemed a remote prospect. Russian forces still occupied the heart of Europe even as the Central European nations (until then usually called Eastern European) were rapidly reorienting themselves toward the West. The last former Soviet troops left Poland in September 1993—several years after the reunification of Germany—and did not depart the Baltic republics until the summer of 1994. Until then, any official public discussion of NATO expansion was premature, though some officials within the Clinton State Department began to promote the idea earlier. At the higher levels, however, the administration regularly deferred to Russian sensitivities. Nonetheless, some strategic thinkers on the outside openly spoke of NATO expansion as the logical and necessary act that would consolidate Europe's new political reality.

Strikingly, when President Walesa expressed a desire for Polish NATO membership, Russian President Yeltsin responded positively. During a visit to Warsaw in August 1993, with Russian troops still in East Germany, Yeltsin publicly stated that he did not view such a prospect as being against Russia's interests. Clinton's top advisers in Russian affairs, as well as his secretary of state, nonetheless urged caution. Thus for the next year or so U.S. efforts concentrated on a process of extensive "preparations" for enlargement, ingeniously labeled the Partnership for Peace, which had the merit of making expansion more likely while delaying the actual decision to expand. In the meantime, Russia's position shifted to open opposition, and by late 1994 Clinton had to reassure Yeltsin by publicly pledging "three no's": no surprises, no rush, and no exclusion of Russia.

Nonetheless, within the Clinton administration the balance gradually shifted to the view that long-range stability in Europe and a healthy American–European relationship could not be attained if a large swath of Europe remained a no-man's land. This conclusion was reinforced by the gradual realization that Russia was undergoing a prolonged crisis that made its long-range conduct inherently unpredictable. That perspective was shared by the newly united Germany, and somewhat less heartily by the British. But it was increasingly contested in the United States by a cluster of former U.S. diplomats, scholars, and pundits who favored some sort of neutral belt in the heart of Europe. In the absence of a strong and clear voice on this subject, and with Clinton personally maintaining an ambiguous posture, the prospect of NATO enlargement appeared to be more doubtful than it actually was.

The issue was further complicated by the increasingly violent conflict in post-Yugoslav Bosnia. Attempts by NATO to dampen that violence, as well as its unprecedented decision to use its airpower against Serbian forces (evoking strong objections from Yeltsin), had a paradoxical effect on the issue of expansion. That NATO's military reaction was necessary to halt—at least temporarily—the hostilities in the geopolitically volatile region spoke for itself. But the fact that Russia—after initially condemning the NATO action—eventually agreed in late 1995 to participate in the Bosnian peace settlement and in the resulting peacekeeping also showed that Russia needed to be involved somehow in a more formal relationship with NATO.

The result was a two-track policy aimed at promoting both a stronger relationship with Russia and a larger NATO. In late 1996, on the eve of the U.S. presidential elections, Clinton publicly committed the United States to the expansion of NATO, and the effort gained momentum following his reelection. His first-term secretary of state gave way to the more dynamic and politically well-connected Madeleine Albright, a protégé of the First Lady (and a friend and former associate of this author). Personally committed to the eastward expansion of NATO, she infused a sense of strategic purpose into the effort.

The two-track process now moved with less hesitation. In May 1997, the NATO-Russia Founding Act was signed, its intent being to reassure Russia that NATO was now a security partner. Clinton again took the opportunity to reiterate America's friendship for Yeltsin's Russia. In July Poland, the Czech Republic, and Hungary were officially invited to join NATO. Invitations to the Baltic republics, Romania, and Bulgaria soon followed. This expansion made Europe's own expansion logical and unavoidable. With the former European Community having redefined itself as the European Union, Europeans themselves decided that it made no sense to exclude their newly democratic neighbors—already tied through NATO to both the United States and the European Union—from actual EU membership. The consummation of that process in the first years of the twenty-first century created—critics notwithstanding—the single most important and cooperative community in world affairs.

The result was the most consequential but also paradoxical accomplishment of the Clinton era. The expansion of NATO and the European Union had not initially been a major priority for Clinton. NATO expansion had little to do with his central preoccupation—globalization—nor did it engage the same emotional commitment as, for example, his attempt to cultivate a personal relationship with Yeltsin. The latter was a personally fulfilling mission; the former was more a matter of strategic duty and an act of historical justice.

Nonetheless, Clinton did it, largely thanks to the zeal of key members of his team and outside promoters who together forced the debate and accelerated the pace. The obvious enthusiasm of the gratified Central Europeans also proved contagious. By the time Clinton stood in front of the Royal Castle in the rebuilt Warsaw in July 1997, announcing to the ecstatic crowds and a triumphant Lech Walesa that Poland and its two Central European neighbors were being invited into the alliance, he was a genuine convert.

Had Clinton been less committed, one can only speculate how uncertain and unstable Europe might have been a decade later—when America and Europe parted ways over Iraq,

FIGURE 3 ❖ EXPANSION OF NATO AND THE EU
AFTER THE END OF THE COLD WAR

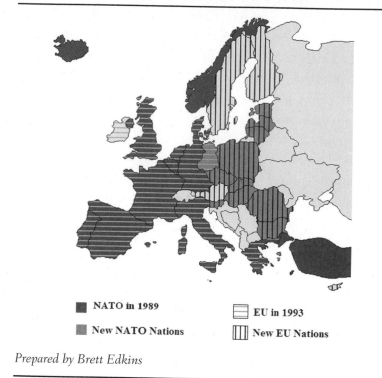

■ NATO in 1989   ☰ EU in 1993

▨ New NATO Nations   ⫿⫿⫿ New EU Nations

Prepared by Brett Edkins

the European drive toward political unity faltered because of internal divisions, and Russia began again to flex its muscles at Ukraine, Georgia, and even the Baltic states and Poland. The Cold War that ended in 1990 could have been revived, in some new form and with a new ideological or territorial twist, if a large swath of postcommunist Europe had remained shut out of the Atlantic community.

The almost coincidental burst of momentum during the 1990s in European construction—including the Treaty of Maastricht, which formally established the European Union; the admission of the previously neutral West European states of Sweden and Finland; the adoption of the euro; the elimination of border controls within the European Union (the Schengen Agreements); and the beginnings of a common European defense policy and an EU rapid reaction force— meant that, in many ways, the last decade of the twentieth century marked the high point in the positive role of the West in world affairs. There was nothing that America and Europe together—the geopolitical superpower and the economic giant with a nascent common political identity—could not do, if they had the will.

And for a while (but—alas—only for a while) that new reality facilitated the joint pursuit of a constructive global agenda in keeping with Clinton's benign and hopefully deterministic view of globalization. The combined influence of America and Europe led to the successful completion in 1994 of the enormously complex web of conflicting trade negotiations known as the Uruguay Round of the General Agreement on Tariffs and Trade. The resulting establishment of the World Trade Organization on January 1, 1995, marked a major step toward the emergence of a global economic order in keeping with the growing sense of supranational solidarity. That the WTO included an institutionalized mechanism for the resolution of conflicting interests, without which the enormous inequalities in human economic conditions could not be addressed, was a significant step forward.

China's subsequent admission to the WTO in 2001—facilitated by several years of patient negotiations pushed by the United States and the European Union—was a further step in the long but essential process of incorporating a potential economic powerhouse into a more cooperative and rule-governed world economic system. China's entry spurred the emergence of the so-called G20—a bloc of developing states led by China, India, South Africa, and Brazil. The economically weaker states thus gained for the first time some genuine political clout in the continuing negotiations for a more equitable global trade system. Clinton's assertion that globalization "cannot be reversed" was thus being validated.

China's accession, however, came with a political price. To facilitate the progressive integration of China's economy into the world system, the United States in 1994 extended most favored nation status to China but waived the usual human rights stipulations. Clinton, with some reluctance, made that decision, reasoning that in the longer run a China that accepts international rules and is drawn into greater interdependence would inevitably be drawn into growing respect for human rights. Globalization, he rationalized, would eventually redress the morally troubling concession.*

While China's growing entanglement in global interdependence was a net plus, two other developments on Clin-

---

*That Clinton was troubled by this issue and personally agonized over it was reflected in the degree to which he reached out for advice, even to outsiders. I was on a beach in Hawaii, returning to the United States from a trip to China, when I received a phone call from the president, who wanted to know whether it would make sense to impose targeted sanctions, for example, on industries controlled by the Chinese army.

ton's watch were potentially more troubling for the Atlantic community's long-run role in world affairs: the financial crisis in Asia and the growing cleavage between America and Europe regarding the scope of supranational rules.

The severe liquidity crisis in Southeast Asia of 1997, set in motion by a deepening Japanese financial malaise and sparked by massive real estate and currency speculation (including an assault by American currency traders on Thailand's foreign exchange reserves), spread rapidly to Taiwan and South Korea. The United States was initially slow to respond, but in early 1998 the U.S. Treasury secretary, Robert Rubin, led an effort that resulted in belated stabilization. Nonetheless, a consensus developed in Asia that the crisis was largely America's fault.

The fact that many blamed the policies of the U.S.-dominated International Monetary Fund for the crisis, combined with China's relatively cautious but constructive conduct (including its decision not to devalue its currency), spurred growing East Asian interest in some form of regional cooperation, with China and/or Japan in the lead and with the region less dependent financially on the United States and European Union.

The second development, disillusioning for those who hoped effective American leadership would shape a world subject to common rules, was the emerging divergence between America and Europe regarding supranational rules. The United States obstructed such politically sensitive agreements as the Ottawa Treaty banning land mines (rejected on the militarily legitimate grounds that U.S. forces in South Korea had deployed a comprehensive barrier of mines along the armistice line for purely defensive purposes) and the Rome Statute for the new International Criminal Court (ICC), which could have made U.S. military personnel subject to international prosecution for war crimes. Clinton actually signed the latter treaty in the waning days of his presidency but did not submit it for ratification. It would certainly have failed in a Congress increasingly dubious of Clinton's views.

Even more damaging to Clinton's reputation as a visionary leader was the failure of the United States to support the international effort to mount a common response to the growing threat of global warming. The Kyoto Protocol, the product of prolonged negotiations in the mid-1990s, became the object of a largely partisan domestic debate in the United States and was openly opposed by major economic interests. In mid-1997, in a shot across Clinton's bow, the U.S. Senate approved, by an astounding 95 to 0 vote, a resolution opposing the protocol on the grounds that it was neither practical nor fair. Though Vice President Gore, the main American advocate of the protocol, signed it on America's behalf in late 1998, Clinton, correctly gauging the public mood, let the issue drift.

By the end of the Clinton era, the hopeful agenda of his presidency was much in doubt. Only the expansion and consolidation of the Atlantic community stood out as a lasting strategic achievement. But its capacity to project a common global purpose was already waning, and soon afterwards it would be severely damaged by the unilateralism of Clinton's successor. But Clinton's central vision—globalization as the "economic equivalent of a force of nature"—was under intense assault. Antiglobalization sentiments fueled incipient anti-Americanism, and at the third WTO ministerial, held in 1999 in Seattle, mass demonstrations physically prevented a new round of multilateral trade negotiations.

America was also becoming more skeptical about far-eaching global cooperation. For a growing number of Americans, supranationality became a highly suspect notion. The Republican party had scored major successes in congressional elections at the midpoint of Clinton's first term (1994), and the "Gingrich revolution" spoke in strident nationalist tones. The resulting challenge to the president's leadership was compounded by his personal difficulties. His credibility was damaged by the prolonged scandal that dominated much of Washington's political life (and most of its private chatter) for a full year, from early 1998 to early 1999, seriously impairing Clinton's ability to mobilize his own constituency.

Ironically, the changing complexion of American politics and the simultaneous decline in Clinton's personal standing provide historically painful validation of Clinton's notion that "foreign affairs is a continuation of domestic politics by other means." As American domestic politics asserted itself with a vengeance, Clinton's once idealistic agenda became increasingly its victim.

Confronting the Past

Many of the global problems Clinton faced had deep-seated origins. Entrenched interests, national rivalries, cultural hedonism of the rich, intense resentments of the poor, and self-righteous ethnic and religious antagonisms stood in the way of translating America's global supremacy into benign action. Coping with such ugly but enduring realities required the use of traditional power instruments not quite in keeping with lofty sentiments. This could only be done with strong domestic support, mobilized on behalf of a clear strategic vision.

Coping with the legacies of the past required Clinton to confront some of the same actors he had dealt with on European unification and nuclear proliferation. Russia was again a concern and European nationalism roared violently to life in the Balkans, while the Middle Eastern stalemate reflected the intransigence of deeply rooted ethnic and religious antagonisms. The end of the Cold War had lifted the lid on many long-simmering local conflicts, which now erupted suddenly and intensely.

Almost immediately after assuming office, Clinton faced outbreaks of violence in several parts of the world. These events diverted him from his agenda and forced him to confront the painful prospect of having to spill blood. Brutal chaos swept Somalia and Rwanda in Africa; Yugoslavia's disintegration escalated into bloody violence almost in the center of the new Europe; Russia soon got bogged down in a war with Chechnya; China probed the limits of America's determination to protect Taiwan from military assault. Moreover, the Middle East festered throughout Clinton's two terms, with little progress and some serious setbacks in the Israeli–Palestinian peace process, with Iraq a source of periodic confrontation, and with anti-U.S. terrorism intensifying along with the region's rising political temperature.

In almost all of these cases, Clinton's first instinct was a reluctance to be involved. These issues did not rank high on his agenda; they engaged neither his idealism nor his intellectual inclinations. They smacked of the ugly past and he knew that coping effectively with them required either jawboning or the use of force. Some of them, such as the conflict in Chechnya, required the abandonment of fond hopes and the contemplation of ugly realities. Last but not least, overcoming perhaps the most entrenched difficulty—the Israeli–Palestinian conflict—raised the risk of increased domestic political difficulties.

These challenges required much more than faith in the historical momentum of globalization or a conviction that world politics could be handled as a continuation of domestic politics. Clinton's critics charged, legitimately, that "globaloney" is no substitute for geostrategy. And geostrategy calls for a design that prioritizes geopolitical challenges in order to facilitate prompt and decisive responses. That kind of measured American leadership was just not there.

To his credit, and despite his personal disinclination, Clinton did try to mount a response in the case of the Balkan crisis, and in the end he was successful. Unfortunately, that cannot be said of Somalia and Rwanda. Shortly after assuming power, Clinton was faced by escalating violence in Somalia, where his predecessor had deployed a small U.S. military force under international sanction on a peacekeeping mission. But in a highly publicized shootout in late 1993, popularized as *Black Hawk Down,* a desperate U.S. military effort to rescue a beleaguered and surrounded Special Forces team in the heart of Mogadishu resulted in heavy U.S. fatalities. Clinton then precipitously terminated the American deployment in Somalia. The contrast between U.S. involvement in the former Yugoslavia and its reticence in Africa was not lost on others.

The impression of America's indifference to Africa was compounded by its prolonged passivity regarding the genocidal calamity raging in Rwanda from 1994 to 1995. The international community essentially just watched. The newly independent African states were unwilling to act, and former European colonial powers intervened only minimally. The United States seemed to take the view that the issue had no wider geopolitical ramifications and was something the Africans themselves, perhaps with help from the former European colonial powers, had to resolve.

In contrast, Clinton eventually acted with greater resolve and efficacy in response to the Balkan crisis, the incipient phase of which he inherited from Bush. The United States had at first been slow in recognizing how potentially explosive multinational Yugoslavia really was. While the reunited Germany promptly recognized (and quietly welcomed) the independence of Slovenia and Croatia, France and Russia, motivated by traditional affinity for Serbia, did not. These conflicting circumstances quickly led to a war over Bosnia, inhabited by a mixture of Catholic Croats, Muslim Bosnians, and Serbian Orthodox Bosnians. Bush's secretary of state, James Baker, was widely quoted as saying, with stunning indifference, "We don't have a dog in this fight."

The war promptly escalated into atrocities not seen in Europe since the end of World War II, including the mass executions committed by Serbian forces in Srebrenica, which aroused Western public opinion. Worried about the negative repercussions, Clinton's national security adviser bluntly warned his boss (according to reporter Robert Woodward) that "the administration's weak, muddle-through strategy in Bosnia was becoming a cancer on Clinton's entire foreign policy—spreading and eating away at its credibility." Before long, America's initial hesitations and the divisions among the Western powers were overcome, in part because ongoing efforts to invigorate the Atlantic alliance, widen NATO, and facilitate the expansion of the European Union created a felicitous atmosphere for a common stand.

Despite angry protests by Russia and the continued reluctance of some European allies, a brief but intense NATO air campaign against Serbia-backed forces compelled a cease-fire. This was followed in late 1995 by a peace conference held in Dayton, Ohio, symbolically underscoring America's central role in resolving the crisis. That resolution, however, did not end the violence, which soon erupted anew over Kosovo, a largely Albanian-populated part of the residual post-Yugoslavia. The Serbian policy of ethnic cleansing directed against the Albanian majority in Kosovo, intended to consolidate a nationally cohesive Serbia, again involved widespread civilian killings and brutal expulsions.

This time the United States acted more decisively, with Secretary Albright taking the lead on behalf of the U.S. government. She effectively exploited the political momentum generated by NATO's expansion to fashion a political coalition in favor of confronting Serbia with a clear-cut choice: leave Kosovo or be forcibly expelled. With America and Europe firmly in step, a sustained bombing campaign inflicted serious damage on Serbia's infrastructure (including its capital) while a NATO expeditionary corps was assembled in Albania and Greece in preparation for a decisive land campaign.

Russia, which objected strongly to this action, made a last-minute attempt to inject itself into the conflict by suddenly deploying a small force into the airport at Pristina, Kosovo's capital, perhaps in an effort to salvage a piece of Kosovo for Serbia or obtain a purely Russian zone of occupation in Kosovo. But with NATO politically determined, the effort came to naught. The policy of expanding and reinforcing the Atlantic community thus proved its worth, and the terminal phase of the Yugoslav crisis was resolved by mid-1999 on Western terms and under American leadership. Serbia was compelled to vacate Kosovo.

Clinton's decision to send troops to Bosnia, made in the face of a Republican-sponsored congressional resolution, and then again to use force to compel Serbia's withdrawal from Kosovo, was critical to the stabilization of the former Yugoslavia. It also fostered successful American–European cooperation in joint security operations. In 2004, after Clinton had left office, the American-led NATO force in Bosnia was transformed into a European-led force, a testimonial to transatlantic ties.

But Clinton's policy toward Russia itself, already strained by NATO's expansion, was greatly complicated by the Yugoslav crisis. Like his predecessor, Clinton put very high emphasis on his personal relationship with Yeltsin, whom he chose to endorse warmly and praise publicly as a committed democrat. Given the political turmoil within Russia, the freefall of its economy, and its financial crisis, it made sense to cultivate a leader who explicitly disowned Russia's imperial past and pledged himself to democracy. Moreover, economic and financial assistance was a way to compensate Russia for its humiliating loss of power over the Central Europeans.

Clinton and his principal advisers on Russia had made a genuine and comprehensive American–Russian reconciliation their major strategic objective. But Russia's severe financial crisis of 1998 brought to the surface the inherent conflict between the blatantly self-enriching economic reformers (and their various American partners) and the resulting outrage among a Russian population drastically impoverished by the ongoing financial upheaval. The U.S.-led IMF effort to bail out the country's collapsing financial structure mainly facilitated the flight of Western investors and speculators. The result was a profound shift in the Russian psyche toward self-sufficient economic nationalism and the discrediting of the Yeltsin regime.

For a Kremlin suffering a loss of status, the hardest pill to swallow was the independence of states that had been part of imperial Russia, long before the 1917 revolution. American support for Ukrainian independence was especially sensitive for Moscow, since without Ukraine Russia could not hope to restore its Slavic empire. For the time being, however, there was not much Russia could do about Ukraine's independence. Chechnya was a different matter. A small non-Russian nation located in the central Caucasus, Chechnya was long repressed but had persistently sought its freedom. In 1944 Stalin had deported almost the entire Chechen population to Kazakhstan, where half of them perished. They were not allowed to return to their homes until the 1960s. Shortly after the Soviet Union dissolved in 1991, the Chechens declared national independence.

The first war between Chechnya and Russia erupted in 1995 after numerous reciprocal provocations and some bloody clashes, including abortive Russian efforts to regain control of Chechnya through local proxies armed by Russian security forces. It lasted for about a year, with the Chechens ferociously defending their independence. A tenuous cease-fire broke down in the wake of Chechen efforts to promote the independence of other peoples in the Caucasus. In late 1999, Yeltsin handed over his increasingly ineffective presidency to his prime minister, Vladimir Putin, who then resumed the war with far greater ferocity for the next several years. In the process, upward of 25 percent of the Chechen population perished, with both sides resorting to terrorist tactics.

We will never know if a more active U.S. effort at mediation would have produced some sort of a compromise formula, particularly at the time of the first Russo–Chechen war. The fact is that Clinton chose to remain indifferent, even comparing the war to the American Civil War, and Yeltsin to Abraham Lincoln. As it happened, the war set in motion the progressive strengthening within the still-turbulent Russian political system of the traditional instruments of Russian power—the security forces and the military. It also created a public atmosphere congenial to reversing Russia's early progress toward democracy. Putin made winning the war his central objective. By identifying his presidency with the energetic pursuit of victory, he was able to exploit rising Russian nationalism, as well as growing resentment of America's global influence, to promote the emergence of a more authoritarian and nationalistic Russian state. Clinton's genuinely fond dream of a comprehensive American–Russian reconciliation was not to be.

Clinton, however, deserves credit for an initiative that subsequently has become an obstacle to a resurgence of Russian imperialism: the U.S.-sponsored Baku-Çeyhan oil pipeline. The effect of that pipeline is to gain for the West direct access to Caspian and Central Asian oil. In October 1995 I was asked by Clinton and his national security adviser—presumably because I had earlier advocated such a U. S. initiative— to deliver a personal letter from Clinton to President Guydar Aliyev of Azerbaijan and to engage him in a dialogue regarding the long-range benefits to Azerbaijan of such a pipeline. A favorable Azeri decision would have required the rejection of ongoing Russian demands that all Azeri oil be exported exclusively through Russian territory. Aliyev and I met for several late-night sessions while during daylight the Azeri president was confronting a high-powered Russian delegation pressing for an exclusive commitment in Russia's favor. Before leaving Baku, I was able to report to Clinton Azerbaijan's commitment to the U.S. initiative and to make a public statement to that effect prior to my departure. Today, the Baku-Çeyhan pipeline is an important contributor to Europe's (as well as America's) efforts to diversify its energy sources.

Clinton faced fewer obstacles in seeking a modus vivendi with China and used the gradual inclusion of China in the WTO to that end. There were two passing crises in the Taiwan Straits in the mid-1990s, with the Chinese—genuinely worried that Taiwan might declare its independence with

U.S. backing—deliberately testing American resolve by seeking to provoke Clinton into a firm reiteration of the commitment made by Presidents Nixon and Carter to a one-China policy. By deploying the U.S. Navy into the Straits, Clinton demonstrated that the United States would not be passive if military hostilities broke out, but at the same time the United States reaffirmed its earlier understanding that the eventual reunification of China and Taiwan is a matter for the Chinese to resolve, provided the resolution does not involve the use of force.

A subsequent exchange of top-level visits (none as personally warm as the Clinton–Yeltsin encounters) restored normalcy to the relationship, despite fears of a rising and hostile China propagated in the Republican-controlled Congress and by some in the mass media. The Clinton administration was generally able to dampen the more extreme notions of an inevitable American–Chinese collision while continuing its efforts to draw China into binding international commitments. Nonetheless, the earlier military confrontation probably did spur increasing Chinese efforts to modernize their forces so that they would eventually be able to challenge American control over the waters separating China from Taiwan.

Perhaps Clinton's most disappointing and fateful legacy was his failure to exploit the fleeting opportunities that surfaced on at least two occasions regarding the stalemated Israeli–Palestinian relationship, and perhaps once regarding Iranian–American relations as well. The first opportunity to push for Israeli–Palestinian peace arose shortly after Clinton assumed office; the second occurred shortly before he left it. The intervening years were wasted while U.S. policy gradually drifted from impartial commitment to a fair settlement to an increasingly one-sided pro-Israel posture.

Clinton's Middle East team reflected that evolution. As time passed, the key officials charged with negotiating the Israeli–Palestinian settlement were increasingly recruited from pro-Israeli research institutes and the Israeli lobbies. Though not of a single mind, the more prominent among them opposed any specific U.S. peace initiative, "an American peace plan," on the grounds that time had to pass before both sides would be ready for a genuine settlement. That argument, however, played into the hands of the more rigid Israeli elements who used the time to expand and consolidate Israeli settlements in the occupied territories, in the belief that "accomplished facts" would eventually force the Palestinians into more one-sided concessions.

The earlier opportunity arose after the Oslo Accords were signed on September 13, 1993, in a formal—and for Clinton personally triumphant—ceremony on the White House lawn, which culminated in the historic handshake between Prime Minister Rabin and Yasser Arafat, the PLO leader. The accords provided for the establishment of de facto Palestinian self-rule in the occupied territories and thus served as the point of departure for an eventual two-state solution implicitly based on the 1967 armistice lines. At the September ceremony, Arafat renounced "the use of terrorism and other acts of violence," but Rabin made no corresponding pledge to halt the construction of settlements in Palestinian territory.

Within a year, the accords were followed by the Israeli–Jordanian Peace Treaty, which meant that Israel now had normal relations with two of its three immediate Muslim neighbors.

The years 1993 to 1995 were thus a moment of opportunity. The Israeli settlements on Palestinian lands were still sparsely populated, and Rabin and Arafat were in effective control of their respective sides. With the two men developing a cool but constructive working relationship, prospects for peace were on the rise. The following year they shared the Nobel Peace Prize.

That hopeful state of affairs came to a sudden end on the night of November 4, 1995, when an Israeli right-wing fanatic assassinated the war hero Prime Minister Rabin. In less than a year, the Israeli government was in the hands of an outspoken critic of the accords, Benjamin Netanyahu, a committed and rather demagogic promoter of more settlements whose credibility some of Clinton's associates found questionable. The peace process took a dramatic downward slide, expansion of Israeli settlements accelerated, and Palestinian acts of violence became more frequent. Not surprisingly, a halfhearted U.S. effort at mediation in October 1998 proved fruitless.

The second opportunity came late in the Clinton presidency, during the last half year of his second term. The Israeli prime minister was again a former war hero, Ehud Barak, the head of the more conciliatory Labor Party. His election in mid-1999 revived the possibility of renewing the peace process, and Barak quite explicitly presented himself in his victory speech as the legatee of Rabin's determination to resolve the Israeli–Palestinian conflict. But with neither the Israelis nor the Palestinians able to resolve on their own the conflicting issues of territory, control of Jerusalem, and the right of return for Palestinian refugees, by mid-2000 both sides were again embroiled in rising tensions and mutual recriminations. At that point Clinton decided to go for broke: to convene a meeting of the principals at Camp David (much as President Carter had done more than twenty years earlier) to help the Israelis and Palestinians find a way out of their long and mutually painful conflict.

But unlike Carter's meeting, Camp David II lacked a dominant U.S. framework, based on independently defined U.S. positions and a U.S. negotiating draft. The negotiations were much more informal and flexible, with the American and Israeli sides alternating in making informal, often just verbal proposals as the discussion fluctuated. At one point, Clinton read out what came to be called the "Clinton parameters": an outline of the specific principles for territorial accommodation and for some sharing of Jerusalem, especially of the respective Jewish and Muslim holy sites. These could have served as the basis for a genuine settlement had there been more time for follow-up and less emphasis on immediately assigning blame for the parties' failure to emerge from the meeting with an agreement in hand.

That Clinton set forth his parameters was nonetheless momentous and remarkable. Momentous because, for the first time, the American side actually presented at the highest level its view of the key components of a fair accommodation. Remarkable because to that point the key players on Clinton's negotiating team had largely opposed any such American initiative. But to their credit they helped Clinton put forward a bold formula, which could appeal to moderate Israelis and Palestinians for an eventual peace based on compromise and not conquest.

What happened next is subject to dispute. Arafat came to be widely blamed for refusing what was publicly presented as a generous Israeli offer; the Palestinian side claimed the offer was never spelled out formally with maps, either by the Americans or the Israelis. Barak's foreign minister later said that if he had been Arafat he would have rejected the proposal as too vague. Clinton generally leaned toward the Israeli version, especially because Arafat had refused to consider the unprecedented compromise formula for some sharing of Jerusalem that Clinton offered.

Moreover, with the U.S. presidential elections approaching and Vice President Gore anxious that any impression of pressure on Israel might hurt his chances in key states, the American side joined in the media campaign to pin the failure exclusively on Arafat. The Palestinian leader made the effort easier by presenting his objections in an essentially negative cast. His demands for specific clarifications and his argument that he had to consult with other Muslim leaders regarding the sharing of Jerusalem implied a "no" more than a "yes." As a result, the disappointing outcome was widely perceived in America as a Palestinian rejection of a joint American–Israeli peace effort. With both U.S. and Israeli elections approaching, this perception was politically expedient.

Had the effort to achieve a breakthrough to peace been undertaken earlier, shortly after Barak's election, perhaps there would have been time for the dust to settle and for the unconsummated Camp David formula eventually to prevail. As it was, the failure to reach an agreement at Camp David was followed shortly by new violence precipitated by Barak's political rival, Ariel Sharon, who conducted a provocative, police-escorted visit to Jerusalem's Haram al-Sharif, a sacred site for

Muslims. The violence produced Palestinian casualties and led to the eruption of the second intifada.

Nonetheless, peace efforts continued. Just before the U.S. presidential elections, negotiations resumed in Sharm el-Sheik but proved inconclusive. Clinton and Arafat met once more, and direct Israeli–Palestinian talks were again renewed in late January 2001 in Taba. Despite some progress, they stalled because of approaching Israeli elections. Clinton was by then a former president, and within days Barak was also out of office, replaced by Sharon, an outspoken critic of Barak's peace efforts.

Since Arafat had been involved in these continued talks, it is reasonable to speculate that had Sharon not won, the peace process might have been renewed. But Sharon won because the violence of the intifada was inflaming Israeli public opinion. In turn, the intifada might not have happened if Sharon had not staged his intrusion on the Temple Mount in order to discredit Barak's peace effort. And that high-profile visit might not have taken place if Israeli elections were not approaching and the Israeli right-wing had not been anxious to discredit Barak's peace gamble. Before long, in the wake of the right-wing electoral victory, getting rid of Arafat became a goal to be pursued in the name of peace jointly by Barak's successor in Israel and by Clinton's successor in America.

Throughout these inconclusive eight years of American involvement in Israeli–Palestinian relations, the issue of Iraq lingered on. The Clinton administration periodically ordered limited air strikes against Saddam's military assets and more than doubled the number of U.S. troops in Saudi Arabia (providing grist for the mills of the anti-American fundamentalists, notably Osama bin Laden). In America itself, in a foretaste of things to come, neoconservative figures began to campaign for unilateral military action to remove Saddam from power. In June 1998 Clinton received a strong plea (made public) to that effect from eighteen vigorous advocates of military intervention, who urged him to "act decisively" to preempt Iraq's possible acquisition of weapons of mass destruction before it was too late. (About two-thirds of the signers became officials in the next administration.)*

Relations with Iran, meanwhile, remained frozen in mutual hostility. Clinton's diplomatic choices were limited by legislation emerging from a Congress politically hostile to him and thus susceptible to initiatives promoted by lobbies with an interest in preventing any exploratory U.S.–Iranian dialogue. In 1995, in response to an Iranian overture opening its oilfields to U.S. investment, President Clinton announced in a speech to the World Jewish Congress the issuance of two executive orders banning trade with Iran. In 1997 Iranian elections produced a surprisingly large majority for more moderate elements, and for a brief period a window of opportunity to explore an improvement in U.S.–Iranian relations may have been open. Fearing domestic political repercussions from Israeli– and Iranian–American lobbies, Clinton again chose not to react positively. Before long, the political balance in

---

*The signatories were Elliott Abrams, Richard L. Armitage, William J. Bennett, Jeffrey Bergner, John Bolton, Paula Dobriansky, Francis Fukuyama, Robert Kagan, Zalmay Khalilzdad, William Kristol, Richard Perle, Peter W. Rodman, Donald Rumsfeld, William Schneider Jr., Vin Weber, Paul Wolfowitz, R. James Woolsey, and Robert B. Zoellick.

Iran tipped back toward fundamentalist and fiercely anti-American elements.

Taken together, these developments produced a basic reversal in the region's prevailing view of America. Many Muslims viewed America's political entry into the Middle East after World War II as a liberating force contributing to the demise of Anglo–French colonial domination. Five decades later, a growing number of Arabs, Egyptians, and Iranians were becoming increasingly receptive to the argument that the region was again suffering foreign domination in a new guise.

Many factors contributed to this emerging resentment: persistent, religiously propagated Iranian hostility for America; inflammatory international reports of growing mortality among Iraqi children caused by U.S.-imposed sanctions in response to Saddam's noncompliance with the post-1991 inspections; and the continuing Israeli–Palestinian conflict, in which U.S. policy was increasingly seen as dedicated more to the preservation of the status quo than to the promotion of a fair peace. All of this contributed to rising political and religious hostility in the region toward America.

That intensifying sentiment in turn provided impetus for the increasingly frequent and lethal terrorist acts directed at U.S. military and diplomatic personnel in the region. Moreover, at least one major terrorist act was attempted during the 1990s in the United States itself: the failed effort to blow up the World Trade Center in New York. Al Qaeda had thus made its presence felt on American soil. The Clinton administration retaliated by bombing al Qaeda's alleged base of operations in Sudan and later some sites in Afghanistan, by then firmly in the hands of the Taliban and offering shelter to al Qaeda.

But there is little in the record to show that the rising terrorist threat and intensifying anti-Americanism precipitated any serious U.S. effort to formulate a comprehensive preemptive strategy. Such an enterprise would have required mobilizing the Arab ruling elites in a common mission to expose and eliminate terrorists, and also to isolate them socially and religiously. The general geopolitical stalemate in the region, largely propitiated by America, discouraged any such efforts, and there is little evidence that serious thought was given in Washington as to what an antiterrorist effort ought to entail. The issue remained largely dormant until American public opinion was shocked into a sudden awakening one horrendous morning seven-and-a-half months after Clinton's departure from office.

Clinton thus left office with Israeli–Palestinian relations in a worse condition and the Middle East more volatile than when he had stepped into it. Unfortunately, his casual foreign policy decision-making system, contaminated by a domestic political calculus, induced a strategic timidity that had dangerous implications for America's long-term interests. Had Clinton succeeded in bringing the Israeli–Palestinian conflict to a constructive and fair closure, he would have earned for himself—and, more importantly, for America—a truly momentous historical success.

America's ascendancy to its solitary perch on the top of the global totem pole occurred around 1990. By 1995 the nation's global status was probably at its peak. The world had accepted the new reality and much of mankind even welcomed it. American power was not only seen as unquestionably dominant but also legitimate, and America's voice was credible.

For that, Clinton deserves credit. If American supremacy took off in 1990, America's global prestige was at its historical apogee by the second half of the decade.

Clinton also deserves major credit for a domestic success that did not involve foreign policy as such but had major foreign policy implications. His economic and financial stewardship transformed the ominously escalating budget deficits of earlier administrations into large surpluses. That turnaround gave a dramatically appealing gloss to America's new global standing. The American model was now seen as a successful fusion of effective political guidance and free enterprise, worthy of international emulation. The contrast with the failed Soviet economy, the tepid growth of some Western European countries, and the burst Japanese bubble enhanced America's primacy and Clinton's standing as Global Leader II.

Clinton himself was admired and almost universally liked, with a personal appeal comparable to that of Franklin Roosevelt and John Kennedy. But he did not exploit his eight years in the White House to commit America's newly acquired global leadership to a definable course that other nations would be inspired to follow. He never made a concerted effort to develop, articulate, and pursue a comprehensive strategy for a responsible American role in the volatile world that confronted him. He had the intellect and the personality to do so. But his casual and politically opportunistic style of decision making was not conducive to strategic clarity, and his faith in the historical determinism of globalization made such a strategy seem unnecessary.

As a result, the global totem pole atop which Clinton stood tall rested on shaky ground. To be sure, when Clinton left office, America was still safely dominant and respected, allied relationships were essentially healthy, and compelling emphasis had been placed on international efforts to remedy the grossly unfair aspects of the human condition. But by the end of the last decade of the twentieth century the rising wave of hostility against America was no longer confined to the Middle East. Even some of its allies were beginning to resent the U.S. hyperpower. Nuclear proliferation was spreading after eight years of inconsequential negotiating and futile protest. Good intentions increasingly failed to compensate for the lack of a clear and determined strategy.

In the meantime, Clinton's charisma at home had lost some of its glow, not only because of his personal difficulties but also because of rising popular sentiment against the proposition that global leadership requires some degree of social self-denial. Social hedonism, bred by domestic economic success, was not congenial to the notion that global leadership might require some sacrifice of personal privilege or some limits on national sovereignty. Supranational cooperation and globalization were thus increasingly questioned by Americans themselves. Though impressively victorious both in the 1992 and the 1996 presidential elections, Clinton's party lost control of Congress to the Republicans in 1994, never to regain it during his presidency. Congressional support for tax cuts for the well-to-do and for a more narrowly defined national interest reflected a degree of social self-indulgence that negated any efforts to use America's moral and political capital on behalf of a wider global commonweal.

Overall, Global Leader II did not leave a historically grand imprint on the world. Complacent determinism, personal shortcomings, and rising domestic political obstacles over-came his good intentions. It was an inconclusive and vulnerable legacy that Clinton bequeathed in 2001 to his doctrinally antithetical successor.

5

Catastrophic Leadership

(and the Politics of Fear)

> This crusade, this war on terrorism is going to take a while. September 16, 2001

> If you are not with us, you are against us.
> Repeatedly, after September 11, 2001

> There are quiet times in the life of a nation when little is expected of its leaders. This isn't one of those times. This is a time that needs—when we need—firm resolve and clear vision and a deep faith in the values that make us a great nation. Labor Day, 2004

NEMESIS NIPS AT THE HEELS OF HUBRIS. THE THREE quotes by President George W. Bush are revealing of his view of himself as Global Leader III and of how his leadership was to be exercised. He saw himself bringing "firm resolve and clear vision and a deep faith" to a new global confrontation between good and evil, a confrontation that might even call for a solitary crusade. The implied contrast with his two predecessors could not be sharper: neither the tactical realism of Global Leader I nor the self-indulgent optimism of Global Leader II could save America from destruction at the hands of its mortal enemies.

The events of 9/11 were an epiphany for Bush. After a single day's seclusion, the new president emerged transformed. From now on, he would be the decisive leader of a nation at war confronting a threat that was both immediate and mortal, the commander in chief of the world's only superpower. America would act on its own, irrespective of the views of its allies. Shocked by the crime and concerned about its safety, the American public rallied around the leader.

The strategy that emerged was a blend of the more imperial formulations of the 1991 draft national security document prepared by Defense Department officials in the Bush I administration (many of whom had returned as advisers to Bush II) and the militant notions of the neoconservative worldview, with its special preoccupation with the Middle East. Strategically, the "war on terror" thus reflected traditional imperial concerns over control of Persian Gulf resources as well as neoconservatives' desire to enhance Israel's security by eliminating Iraq as a threat.

The initial results of this combination were certainly conducive to hubris. The Taliban government in Afghanistan, which had provided shelter to al Qaeda, was promptly overthrown by U.S. military intervention, and less than eighteen months later Saddam Hussein's regime in Iraq was destroyed by a U.S. ground offensive in a mere three weeks. The mood in the White House was triumphant. An exuberant President

Bush even teasingly quipped to the new governor of occupied Iraq, "You want to do Iran for the next one?"

The arrogance that swept the Bush White House was captured in a story in *The New York Times Magazine* by Ron Suskind (October 2004) in which a senior Bush aide derisively dismissed criticism from what he called the "reality-based community." Said the official, "That's not the way the world really works anymore. . . . We are an empire now, and when we act, we create our own reality. And while you're studying that reality—judiciously as you will—we'll act again, creating other new realities, which you can study too, and that's how things will sort out. We're history's actors. . . and you, all of you, will be left to just study what we do." One can imagine the daydream that gave rise to this astonishing pronouncement: first Iraq, then Syria, then Iran, then Saudi Arabia. . . .

Not surprisingly, nemesis was not long in coming. In just a few months the foreign policy of the world's first global power became dominated by the draining consequences of a war in a remote country, a war the United States itself had started but could not end. At the same time, the war on terror increasingly took on the menacing overtones of a collision with the world of Islam as a whole. U.S. foreign policy slipped its half-century's mooring in the Atlantic community. Soon it was condemned by much of the world's public opinion. The blend of neocon Manichaeanism and President Bush's newfound propensity for catastrophic decisiveness caused the post–9/11 global solidarity with America to plunge from its historical zenith to its nadir.

There had been little reason to expect such grand historical swings from the new president. His electoral campaign did not seriously address foreign policy issues. Some of his public comments betrayed a basic ignorance of world affairs, quite in contrast with his two predecessors. His first six months as president were not notable for any demonstrable sense of direction in foreign policy. But his criticisms of Clinton's performance were not cast in the neocon mold. Bush's electoral campaign had stressed compassion, the national interest, and the need for a humble foreign policy, guideposts that left wide latitude for interpretation.

His choice of top associates implied continuity with the realism that had characterized Bush I's foreign policy. For his vice president he selected his father's former secretary of defense, Richard Cheney. His secretary of state, Colin Powell, had likewise been a senior official—chairman of the Joint Chiefs of Staff in the Clinton administration—and had also been seen as a potential Republican presidential candidate. Donald Rumsfeld, the secretary of defense, had held the same post under President Ford and likewise had once toyed with running for president.

It was a seasoned team that vastly outranked the new president in seniority and experience, at least until he gained confidence, self-assertiveness, and a sense of mission. The new team initially focused on Bush I's unfinished business: missile defense, military transformation, big-power relationships. Neither proliferation nor terrorism ranked high, and the national security adviser, Condoleezza Rice, even dismissed an early intelligence warning of possible terrorist strikes as largely a "historical" study.

After 9/11, the second layer of the president's team—younger and with stronger neoconservative views—rose eventually to become the intellectual source of his inspiration and self-definition. The critical role was played by three appointees: Rice; I. Lewis Libby, the vice president's chief of staff; and Deputy Defense Secretary Paul Wolfowitz. Rice represented the new generation in the White House. A former staffer for Bush I's National Security Council and an established academic, she had tutored the new president on foreign affairs during the election campaign, establishing a personal bond between them that compensated for her more junior status in her relations with the other principals. Although not identified with any strongly held strategic perspective, she leaned toward a categorical perception of international complexities, congenial to the new president's proclivity for moralistic dichotomies and reinforcing (as well as justifying) his penchant for reductive rhetoric about good and evil.

As national security adviser, she was less effective in coordinating the decision-making system because both the secretary of state and the secretary of defense were more senior and not inclined to defer to her. Moreover, the vice president created his own, smaller equivalent of the NSC, allowing Libby, capitalizing on the close relationship between the president and vice president, to gain bureaucratic clout that cut into Rice's authority. But while it diminished her bureaucratic effectiveness, none of this constrained the president's growing reliance on her to reinforce his increasingly self-confident instincts.

Rice's ideological influence on the president was aided by Wolfowitz and Libby. The latter two had collaborated on the 1991 strategy document, articulating the case for an unadulterated American global military superiority, and both held

strong views regarding the Middle East, specifically Iraq and Israel. Like some of the subordinates they chose for key positions
in the White House and Defense Department, they had in the
late 1990s been among the signatories of letters addressed either to President Clinton or to Prime Minister Netanyahu of Israel, urging a more muscular policy of confrontation with
Saddam Hussein's lingering regime in Iraq. This cluster of people, supported by articulate advocates outside the administration, provided the strategic impetus for the initiative that
unfolded after 9/11 and culminated a year and a half later in
the military invasion of Iraq.

While the full record of the internal deliberations will not
be known until well after the end of the Bush presidency—
through competing recollections and declassification of secret
documents—enough is known already to permit a broad reca-
pitulation of how Bush's response to 9/11 emerged and took
shape. Involved in forming that response—in addition to the
president himself—were his principal domestic political advisers, his imperially minded senior advisers, and the latter's
closest subordinates. These were the principal theorists of a
drastically revised view of America's role in the world.

Bush's principal domestic political advisers seized on the
9/11 event as an opportunity to claim the political high
ground. By elevating the criminal attack into an allegorical
declaration of war, they anointed the president with the status of a "wartime" commander in chief endowed with enhanced executive authority. Appealing to the public's
outraged patriotism while propagating fear and paranoia,
they calculated, would yield political benefits, and the results of the 2004 election bore them out. The endless war

on terror thus became a domestic political tool as much as a foreign policy.

Among members of the foreign policy team, an overwhelming consensus naturally favored a muscular response. There was unanimous agreement on America's need—and right—to eliminate the Taliban regime in Afghanistan that had sheltered the central perpetrators of the 9/11 outrage. This position also commanded almost universal international support. A cleavage, however, developed over what to do next. Within days of 9/11, the outspoken and highly motivated Wolfowitz dared to speculate publicly about the need for a follow-up operation against Iraq, but Secretary of State Powell—mindful of the unpredictable risks of a larger war—reacted sharply, stating that the deputy defense secretary spoke only for himself. Unbeknownst to anyone at the time, however, the president took the alleged offender aside and quietly told him to "keep it up, keep it up," revealing his own early predisposition.

Powell's role remained ambiguous. Publicly he was one of the most effective spokesmen for war in Iraq, arguing that it was a necessity dictated by the rising strategic threat posed by Iraq's presumed weapons of mass destruction. Because he was seen as a moderate, his arguments carried more weight than the fire-breathing, sometimes apocalyptic advocacy of the vice president, the national security adviser, and the secretary of defense. Within the NSC, however, he seemed to urge restraint and reliance on international sanctions. And in private, including off the record evening meetings with a nationally prominent journalist, he conveyed deep reservations about the premises and consequences of the course on which the president seemed determined to embark. One has to wonder what might have happened if, instead of sharing his concerns with a writer planning a book, he had chosen to take a public stand on a matter so central to the national interest.

Bush subsequently confirmed in various comments that for him 9/11 was a call to a special mission, a personal epiphany with touches of a divine vocation. This belief gave him a self-confidence bordering on arrogance and inspired a simpleminded Manichaean dogmatism. His speechwriters, some with strong neocon leanings, took advantage of this propensity, infusing into his public statements a penchant for swaggering challenges such as "bring'em on," broad-brush characterizations ("axis of evil"), and occasionally even Islam-ophobic demagogy. One can only surmise that the tradition-ally scrupulous NSC oversight of presidential speech drafts had become dysfunctional.

It is also hard to avoid the conclusion that at some point during 2002 the NSC ceased to perform its traditional role of carefully screening and assessing the flow of intelligence to the president. Alternative or skeptical assessments from other intelligence sources were either slighted or not con-veyed. National Security Adviser Rice herself became a pub-lic cheerleader for the argument that Iraq conclusively had weapons of mass destruction. The NSC thereby became an echo for the views that the politically accommodating direc-tor of Central Intelligence was personally presenting to the president. Vice President Cheney and his chief of staff also pressured CIA analysts, both by pointed questioning and by preemptively (especially in Cheney's case) asserting to the public, as unquestionable facts, conclusions that at best were hypothetical or based on extrapolation. Last but by no means least, the Defense Department created its own intelligence office on Iraq. Run by one of the department's more motivated neocon officials, the office predictably reinforced the conclusions that the president and vice president were publicly espousing.

With the president clearly favoring military action, the vice president embracing the worst-case hypothesis regarding the threat posed by Iraq and its alleged link to al Qaeda, and the second tier relentlessly pressing its strategic advocacy, a de facto consensus in favor of military action emerged by early 2002. By June the vice president was explaining to the nation, in an address before the Veterans of Foreign Wars, the benefits of forcibly removing Saddam Hussein: "Moderates throughout the region would take heart, and our ability to advance the Israeli-Palestinian peace process would be advanced." Even while seeking congressional and U.N. approval for war in late 2002 and early 2003, Bush, in a confidential discussion with Prime Minister Tony Blair recorded by Blair's foreign policy adviser, actually toyed with the idea of staging a deliberate military provocation in order to precipitate a casus belli. For a president, even to raise such a notion is to skate on thin legal ice.

For the next three or four years the top-level obsession with Iraq overshadowed every other foreign policy issue America faced. The consequences of Bush's decisive leadership have not been trivial.

INTERNATIONAL CHRONOLOGY: JANUARY 2001 TO PRESENT

2001. Bush looks into Putin's soul during their first meeting in Ljubljana. U.S.–Chinese incident over spy plane sparks tensions. Kyoto Protocol not submitted to U.S. Congress for ratification. World Trade Center in New York City destroyed and the Pentagon in Washington, D.C., damaged in terrorist suicide strikes. War on terror declared. NATO steps forward with collective defense commitment in support of America. United States intervenes militarily to overthrow the Taliban regime in Afghanistan. Doha Round trade negotiations begin. China joins the WTO. Pakistan and India on the brink of war.

2002. Conflict erupts in Darfur. Bush labels North Korea, Iran, and Iraq the "axis of evil." U.S. withdraws its signature from the International Criminal Court Treaty. Israeli Prime Minister Ariel Sharon, with U.S. endorsement, crushes the Palestinian Authority and isolates Yasser Arafat. Bush then calls for creation of a Palestinian state. U.S. withdraws from the ABM Treaty. Euro bank notes placed in circulation. Bush obtains congressional and U.N. approval for use of force in Iraq. North Korea rejects IAEA restrictions and asserts that its nuclear facilities are a matter only for North Korea and the U.S. to discuss. Russia begins constructing Iran's first nuclear plant at Bushehr.

2003. Israel begins to build the security wall somewhat beyond the 1967 armistice lines. Turkey refuses to permit U.S. troop deployment for war in Iraq. U.S. swiftly crushes Iraqi forces and occupies Iraq in a war openly opposed by France, Germany, and Russia. Weapons of mass destruction not found in Iraq. North Korea announces withdrawal from the Nonproliferation Treaty. U.S. calls for a regional response but Russia and China block U.N. condemnation of North Korea. NATO assumes command of the International Security Assistance Force in Afghanistan. Agreement announced for Six-Party Talks regarding North Korean nuclear program. Iran promises to suspend uranium enrichment. Libya abandons its nuclear program.

2004. Six-Party Talks begin. Terror bombings in Madrid. Iran reverses its pledge not to enrich uranium. Abu Ghraib scandal erupts. Resistance to U.S. occupation and sectarian strife mount in Iraq. NATO expanded by seven more members, EU by ten. Iran agrees to suspend enrichment as part of a temporary deal with the EU. Orange Revolution prevails in Ukraine. Tsunami devastates Southeast Asian coastline and U.S. mounts major disaster relief.

2005. Kyoto Protocol goes into force, minus the U.S. Secretary of state labels North Korea and Iran "outposts of tyranny." Mahmoud Abbas elected president of the Palestinian Authority, second intifada ends, Israel disengages from Gaza. Ahmadinejad elected president of Iran. London terror bombings occur. North Korea announces possession of nuclear weapons, but Six-Party Talks resume. EU constitution rejected by French and Dutch voters. Iran resumes uranium enrichment. WTO ministerial conference fails to reach agreement on the Doha Round. Sectarian conflict in Iraq intensifies.

2006. Bush accepts India into the nuclear club. American and European negotiators offer Iran a choice of a compromise settlement or sanctions. Violence mounts in Iraq and Palestine, erupts in Lebanon, and resurfaces in Afghanistan.

The "Central Front" as the Cemetery of Neocon Dreams

More than any other war in America's history, the one in Iraq has produced an instant bibliography of informative and revealing books. The historical background, the political decision making, the deliberate manipulation of public anxiety, the strategy and execution of the military campaign, the subsequent chaos and insurgency as well as rising sectarian strife have been described in endless detail. The public's right to know has been satisfied, leaving little excuse for individual ignorance of the war's key aspects. What remains is to make one's own judgment regarding the consequences of this historically controversial undertaking for America's position in the world. (My personal favorites are William Polk, *Understanding Iraq*; George Packer, *The Assassins' Gate*; Michael R. Gordon and Bernard E. Trainor, *Cobra II*; and Anonymous, *Imperial Hubris*.)

By 2006 it was clear that the costs of the war had exceeded its one positive accomplishment: the removal of Saddam Hussein, who in any case had already been rendered impotent anyway. These costs do not call for extensive elaboration because they speak for themselves and are generally familiar.

First, *the war has caused calamitous damage to America's global standing*. America's global credibility has been shattered. Until 2003 the world was accustomed to believing the word of the president of the United States. When he made an assertion of fact, he was presumed to know the facts and tell the truth about them. Yet two months after the fall of Baghdad, Bush was flatly still asserting (in an interview destined for a European audience) that "we found the weapons of mass destruction." As a result, America's capacity to make a credible case on such internationally contentious issues as the Iranian and North Korean nuclear programs suffered grievously.

Distrust has also undermined America's international legitimacy, an important source of the nation's "soft power." Previously America's might was viewed as legitimate because America was seen as somehow identified with the basic interests of mankind. Power viewed as illegitimate is inherently weaker because its application requires a higher input of force to achieve the desired result. Loss of soft power thus reduces "hard power."

America's moral standing in the world, an important aspect of legitimacy, was also compromised by the prisons at Abu Ghraib and Guantanamo, as well as by the increasing number of cases suggesting that demoralization—inherent in the psychological brutality of waging a counterinsurgency in the midst of hostile civilians—is beginning to infect the occupation troops. The brutalities documented at Abu Ghraib and Guantanamo should have implicated the secretary of defense and his deputy for permitting—and perhaps even generating—an atmosphere congenial to such abuse. The lack of subsequent high-level accountability transformed the transgressions by individual soldiers into acts of U.S. statesmanship, staining America's moral escutcheon.

Most important of all, the war has discredited America's global leadership. America was able neither to rally the world to its cause nor to decisively prevail by the use of arms. Its actions have divided its allies, united its enemies, and created opportunities for its rivals and ill wishers. The world of Islam has been stirred into bitter hatred. Respect for American statesmanship has plunged precipitously, while America's capacity to lead has been gravely damaged.

Second, *the war in Iraq has been a geopolitical disaster.* It has diverted resources and attention from the terrorist threat, with the result that initial successes in Afghanistan were followed by a resurgence of the Taliban, creating potential new havens for al Qaeda. A similar trend has developed in Somalia. The political stability of Pakistan remains in doubt, with extremist elements in the country exploiting the regime's close ties to the United States.

The physical toll of the war has been steadily rising. While the number of U.S. dead (approaching 3,000) and maimed (over 20,000) has been carefully registered, the number of Iraqis killed remains deliberately uncounted. It is clearly in the high tens of thousands, not to mention the wounded, and many relatives of those killed blame America for their suffering.

The direct financial costs can be calculated with some accuracy, and these—according to congressional studies—already exceed $300 billion. Indirect costs are several times higher. The implications for America's military power and economic health are obviously adverse.

Contrary to the vice president's predictions, anti-American sentiments have become pervasive throughout the Middle East. Politically radical and religiously fundamentalist forces are gaining popular appeal and endangering regimes friendly to the United States. The destruction of Iraq removed from regional play the only Arab state capable of standing up to Iran, thereby benefiting America's most fervent opponent in the region. In geopolitical terms, the war has been a self-inflicted defeat for America and a net gain for Iran.

Third, *the attack on Iraq has increased the terrorist threat to the United States.* When the first flush of victory had passed ("mission accomplished"!) and it became evident that the core argument of the demagogic case for war was false—there were no WMDs in Iraq—the ongoing conflict was relabeled by none other than the president himself as "the central front in the war on terror." In other words, fighting rebellious Iraqis who oppose the U.S. occupation became the substantive definition of a war that was aimed vaguely at "terror," a technique for killing but hardly an identifiable enemy. And if America were to stop waging that war, the president warned, the Iraqis would somehow cross the Atlantic and wage a terror campaign on American soil.

The war on terror, with no clearly defined enemy but strong anti-Islamic connotations, unified Islamic opinion into growing hostility toward America, thereby creating fertile soil for new recruits to terrorism against either America or Israel. It strengthened the appeal of extremism, infusing political hostility toward foreigners with religious antagonism toward infidels. That in turn made it more difficult for moderate Muslim elites, themselves politically threatened by rising Islamic extremism, to fight terrorist cells by rallying their people against extremist political and religious sentiments.

(In the fall of 2003, a revealing poll asked responders whether they regretted the initial lack of effective Iraqi military resistance—in effect, whether they regretted that more Americans were not killed. The disappointed numbered 93 percent in Morocco, 91 percent in Jordan, 82 percent in

Lebanon, 82 percent in Turkey, 82 percent in Indonesia, 81 percent in Palestine, and 74 percent in Pakistan.)

The peculiar definition of both the war on terror in general and the war in Iraq specifically was rejected from the start by the overwhelming majority of world public opinion. By the end of the war's second year, the majority of the American public had come to share that negative opinion. The palpable absurdity of the new case for war reflected desperation: even diehards in the administration could not fail to note that America's standing in the world had taken a catastrophic dive while the engagement in the alleged central front in the war on terror had become largely an isolated American enterprise.

Three articles of faith, fervently embraced by the administration and derived largely from the neocon worldview, underlie the policy decisions that transformed the initial U.S. military success in Afghanistan into disaster in Iraq. The first was that the acts of terror originating from the Middle East reflected a deep-seated nihilistic rage toward America unrelated to specific political conflicts or recent history. The second was that the political culture of the region, notably of the Arabs, respects force above all else, making the application of raw U.S. (or proxy) power the essential component of a lasting solution to the region's problems. The third, developed somewhat belatedly, was that electoral democracy could be imposed from outside. Arabs could be made to shift from hating freedom to loving it even while subject to culturally and religiously foreign pacification by force.

Contrary to the case often made by Bush himself, the widespread antagonism toward America is not because the region's Muslim's "hate freedom" but because historical memories cause them to resent the increasingly close identification of American power in the region with the British colonial past and Israeli policies of the present. The British record in Iraq in the 1920s and 1930s bears a stunning resemblance to the American performance since 2003: report after report hailing progress in imposing enlightened democratic rule on the natives, followed by belated admissions of failure, with RAF strafing and punitive military action in between. (The British colonial secretary in the early 1920s—Winston Churchill—even urged the RAF to use poison gas bombs against the Iraqi insurgents.)

The current American intervention, however, is being pursued in more difficult times. In the early twentieth century, the Middle East was freshly emancipated from Ottoman rule but still living in the colonial era. Social resentment of foreign rule was not pervasive. Notions of national liberation were confined to narrow elites, and religious passions against outsiders were not yet inflamed. That is no longer the case. American political tutelage is not only unwelcome to most but bitterly resented by many. The less than successful governor of Iraq, Paul Bremer, concluded in his memoir that the U.S. occupation has become "ineffective," but American policy in Iraq remains blind to why that is so.

Compounding the dilemmas of a war waged by an administration lacking historical perspective is the psychological and even visual identification of American conduct with Israeli practices. Televised scenes of heavily armed and individually armored U.S. troops pounding down doors in Iraqi homes,

confronting frightened families, and blindfolding and shack-
ling their males evoked earlier images of Israeli troops doing
exactly the same in occupied Palestine. It did not matter if the
Israelis were often reacting to terrorist acts against Israeli
civilians. To millions of Muslim viewers, the similarity of such
scenes reinforced fanatical al Qaeda charges of collusion between American imperialism and expansionist Zionism, both
allegedly marching in the footsteps of the British colonialists.
Fairly or not, the political effect was to mobilize intense, focused resentments.

The ahistorical character of America's misadventure in Iraq
further highlighted the limitations of a strategy primarily dependent on force. Such reliance was fervently preached by
the strategists who guided British policy in the region, the
French response to the Algerian challenge in North Africa,
and the Israeli reaction to Arab belligerence. Peculiar to all
three has been the view that the Arab mentality is particularly
inclined to respect force and view any willingness to compromise as a sign of weakness. Overwhelming military power has
been repeatedly prescribed as the only reliable tool for resolving conflicts and imposing durable solutions.

There is some rationality to such an argument, provided a
fundamental precondition is met: that one has sufficient
might and treasure to apply force until the other side is
crushed. It is also reasonable to argue that the weaker side
may at some point realize it is facing utter destruction by a
determined, resolute, and more powerful opponent, and that
abject capitulation is the better course of action. The problem for America is that while its power is incomparably

greater than that of any state or religious group in the region, it cannot, for domestic reasons, mobilize on a sufficient scale to impose its will by force throughout the Middle East and beyond.

I have elsewhere described the region from Suez to Xinjiang as the new "Global Balkans": a geopolitically important region of intense ethnic and religious violence driven by a growing political resentment against outside domination, especially when imposed by military forces from religiously and culturally alien societies. The region has a suction effect on major powers. Given that the Global Balkans are inhabited by about 500 million people and that the conflicts in the Middle East are igniting religious and political passions throughout the region, the United States would have to undertake total national mobilization in order to prevail solely through military power.

In brief, the United States faces, but on a much larger scale, the same dilemma that Israel faces regarding its Arab neighbors: each lacks the means to impose an enduring unilateral solution dictated entirely by its own definition of goals and interests. The British wisely understood this and left the Middle East without a prolonged conflict; the French came to understand it only after a protracted and debilitating war in Algeria. America is reluctantly assimilating the same lesson through its current involvement in Iraq and Afghanistan, and potentially elsewhere as well if those two conflicts spread throughout the region.

The notion that the solution to the dilemma confronting America is to impose accelerated democracy in the region is

FIGURE 4 ❖ THE GLOBAL BALKANS

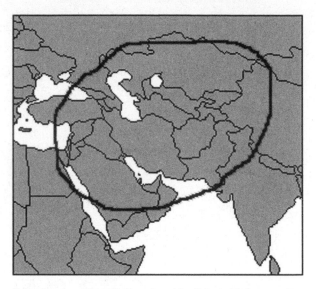

Extending from Egypt's Suez Canal to China's Xinjiang region, from northern Kazakhstan to the Arabian Sea, the Global Balkans of today mirror the traditional Balkans of the nineteenth and twentieth centuries in that they are internally unstable and their geopolitical importance causes foreign rivalries. The contemporary Balkans circled above, inhabited by about 500 million people, are burdened by internal instability derived from ethnic and religious tension, poverty, and authoritarian governments. Ethnic conflict within the Global Balkans involves 5.5 million Jewish Israelis and 5 million Arab Palestinians; 25 million Kurds and their partitioning states of Turkey, Iraq, and Syria; and between India and Pakistan in the dispute over Kashmir, as well as numerous potentially severe ethnic and minority conflicts in Iran and Pakistan. Religious conflicts involve the Muslims and the Hindus, Muslim Shiites versus Sunnis, and a variety of others. In 2005, unemployment was as high as 50 percent in the Gaza Strip, 40 percent in Afghanistan, 25 percent in Iraq, and 20 percent in the West Bank, and 18 percent in Kyrgyzstan.

equally misconceived. Democracy historically has emerged through a prolonged process of enhancement of human rights, first from the economic and then to the political, first among some privileged classes and then on a wider scale. That process in turn entails the progressive appearance of the rule of law, and the gradual imposition of legal and later constitutional rules over the structures of power. In that context, the adoption of free elections leads progressively to the emergence of a system of rule based on fundamental notions of compromise and accommodation, with rules of the game respected by political opponents who do not see their contest as a zero-sum game.

In contrast, when democracy is rapidly imposed in traditional societies not exposed to the progressive expansion of civil rights and the gradual emergence of the rule of law, it is likely to precipitate intensified conflict, with mutually intolerant extremes colliding in violence. That is exactly what short-sighted American efforts to promote democracy have yielded, not only in Iraq but also in Palestine, Egypt, and Saudi Arabia. The result has not enhanced prospects for stability but intensified social tensions. The best such efforts are likely to produce is a fervent but intolerant populism, ostensibly democratic but in fact a tyranny of the majority.

One cannot entirely dismiss the suspicion that the most fervent advocates of "democracy" for the Middle East know this, but see in the promotion of democracy an expedient tool for the eventual imposition of force. Democracy becomes a subversive tool for destabilizing the status quo, leading to an armed intervention that is justified retroactively by the argument that the democratic experiment has failed and that the extremism it produced legitimates the one-sided employment of raw power.

The three basic misconceptions described above should make Americans think very hard about the long-term consequences of an expanding American military involvement in the Global Balkans. What has already occurred in Iraq, and the growing dilemmas that Israel faces as a result of its misguided reliance on similar notions in dealing with its neighbors, provide a foretaste of the kind of difficulties that might dramatically threaten America's global status. The Global Balkans could become the swamp from which America is unable to extract itself.

As the world of Islam is increasingly driven by widespread anti-American passions, other states that see themselves as competitors to America will be tempted to take advantage of America's misguided sense of direction. The emerging partnership between China and Russia on a number of international issues suggests that that risk is hardly remote. The oil producers in the Persian Gulf region, seeking political stability and reliable consumers, may increasingly gravitate toward China. Unlike Bush's America, China emphasizes political stability over democracy and can be a reliable source of reassurance. A political shift of the Middle East away from America toward China would have a ripple effect on Europe's links with America, threatening the primacy of the Atlantic community.

It is therefore a matter of some urgency that America cease to view the "central front" as some sort of unique historical vocation and begin to see it as a lesson from which to draw fundamental revisions of its approach to the Middle East. The

Iraq War in all its aspects has turned into a calamity—in the way it was internally decided, externally promoted, and has been conducted—and it has already stamped the Bush presidency as a historical failure.

Even if the war were somehow to end before President Bush departs, undoing its historical legacy will take enormous effort and much time. Perhaps the war's only saving grace is that it made Iraq the cemetery of neocon dreams. Had the war been more successful, America by now might be at war with Syria and Iran, pursuing a policy driven more by Manichaean notions and dubious motivations than by any sober definition of its national interest.

And the Rest of the World

At the start of Bush's second term, Condoleezza Rice, soon to be shifted from national security adviser to secretary of state, stated in an interview, "When I look at the current period, I recognize that there isn't any such thing as a great architectural design." Having earlier stated that America's response to the lack of international support for its venture in Iraq ought to be to "punish France, ignore Germany, forgive Russia," the president's closest foreign policy adviser thereby conveyed her disdain both for architecture in foreign affairs and for collective allied decision making. That view dominated Bush's first term.

By the time she moved from the White House to the State Department, Rice had ceased being a junior among senior statesmen. Four years at the elbow of a president who had become more self-assured and convinced of his special mission had gradually upgraded her status. Moreover, her appointment as secretary of state took her out of the doctrinaire White House environment and placed her in a department in which it was more widely acknowledged that neither the solitary war in Iraq nor the exaltation of unilateralism as a moral virtue was proving productive.

But before the need for rethinking had sunk in, the administration's policy toward the rest of the world (which commanded much less presidential attention than Iraq) meandered from slogan to slogan with no clear goal or strategy. The absence of either was evident in U.S. policy toward the Israeli–Palestinian conflict, toward Russia and China, and toward the growing risks of nuclear proliferation, as well as in a basic lack of interest in peacekeeping, global poverty, or ecology. All of these issues were overshadowed by the concentration of the president's time, effort, public campaigning, and physical stamina on prevailing in (or at least not losing) the one enterprise that bore his personal imprint.

U.S. global policy thus became skewed and immobilized. Bush's priorities had to change, even if he made no deliberate decision to that effect. Gaining international military support for the Iraqi undertaking, even from the remotest countries and at the most symbolic levels—say, just a platoon—became a major task of U.S. diplomacy. Obtaining credibility for the largely fictitious "coalition of the willing" demanded energy, leverage, and financial inducements. Unlike the Gulf War of 1991, the military campaign in 2003 was largely a solitary and unilateral American undertaking. Except for the British, other national forces' participation in combat was minimal, even though the White House misleadingly claimed in a March

2003 press release that forty-nine states were committed to a coalition "that has already begun military operations to disarm Iraq of its weapons of mass destruction." The facts on the ground were quite otherwise and stood in sharp contrast to the Gulf War of 1991. That war had involved a substantial presence of troops from some Arab states as well as Pakistan, which helped legitimate the invasion within the Muslim world (compare Figure 5 with Figure 2 on page 71).

Beyond destabilizing the Middle East, the Iraq War had a further, much more important consequence. It made the success or failure of U.S. policy in the Middle East the test case of American global leadership. During the Cold War, America's leadership of the free world depended on its performance on the "central front" of that struggle: Europe itself. And America's final victory was won there. America's plunge into Iraq transformed the lingering crisis in the Middle East—allowed to fester under Reagan, Bush, and Clinton—from a chronic problem into a make-or-break challenge. The loss of U.S. dominance in the region would have catastrophic consequences for America's position in Europe and the Far East. Neither America's transatlantic allies nor China and/or Japan, could be indifferent if America's policy in the Middle East were to precipitate a highly radicalized, openly anti-American upheaval that evolved into an Algerian-style protracted campaign of asymmetrical warfare against America and America's client state in the region, Israel. The Middle Eastern states, especially the oil exporters, would have to make their own arrangements, seek new havens for their investments, and carefully solicit protection from rising powers such as China in order to survive in such a turbulent environment.

FIGURE 5

MILITARY PARTICIPATION IN
IRAQ INVASION, MARCH 2003

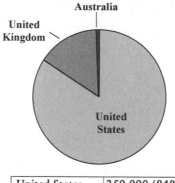

United States	250,000 (84%)
United Kingdom	45,000 (15%)
Australia	2,000 (0.7%)
Poland	200 (0.07%)

MILITARY CONTRIBUTION TO
POST-COMBAT PACIFICATION, AUGUST 2006

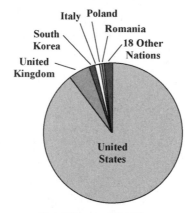

Total Troops: 150,000
Total Non-U.S. Troops: 16,000

Prepared by Brett Edkins

The events of 9/11 did not lead only to Baghdad. They also caused Bush to fundamentally redefine U.S. policy toward the long-lasting, tragic, and increasingly brutal Israeli–Palestinian conflict. Clinton's geopolitically inconclusive but sympathetic partiality toward Israel gave way to overt identification with the Israeli approach, namely, to favor one-sided "accomplished facts" as the basis for eventual resolution. These "facts" quickly came to involve U.S.–Israeli collusion in the removal of Palestinian leader Yasser Arafat from the political scene because he was seen as an obstacle to American–Israeli policy; the application by the Israelis of sustained physical pressure on the Palestinians; U.S. indifference to the continued expansion of the settlements on the West Bank; and the preemptive use of force through targeted assassinations, irrespective of human cost and "collateral damage," in response to Palestinian acts of terrorist outrage.

One such act destroyed an initiative that might have led to a constructive breakthrough in Israeli–Arab relations. In mid-February 2002, the members of the Arab League, prompted by Saudi Crown Prince Abdullah, offered full diplomatic relations with Israel and normal trade relationships as well as security guarantees in return for a peace based on mutual acceptance by the Israeli and Palestinian sides of the June 1967 borders. Within days, any prospect for even a discussion of the offer was derailed by a bloody suicide attack on Israeli civilians. That in turn prompted Prime Minister Sharon to retaliate against the entire Palestinian Authority with violent Israeli military action throughout the West Bank. The Palestinian Authority ceased to function, and Arafat was placed under house arrest (not to reemerge until he was transported to the hospital where he died). President Bush gave full endorsement to the Israeli response, which in effect meant that an autonomous Palestinian partner in the negotiating process ceased to exist.

In return for this U.S.–Israeli political alliance, based on the presumption that a peace will eventually emerge when the weaker side realizes that it has no choice, the United States obtained Israel's acquiescence to an eventual two-state solution involving Israel's coexistence with a new Palestinian state. The formula was formally proposed by President Bush in an address in the White House Rose Garden in June 2002, though the U.S. side refrained from taking a clear-cut position on such difficult issues as the actual territorial settlement and the sharing of Jerusalem. The date for the implementation of this plan was given as 2005, but its parameters—following Israeli preference—were deliberately left vague.

It soon became clear to the region that the Bush–Sharon duet jointly defining U.S. policy was playing for time. With Bush having proclaimed Sharon "a man of peace," the next several years were dominated by halfhearted U.S. peace initiatives, periodic terrorist killings by frustrated Palestinians, lethal retaliation by outraged Israelis, continuing radicalization of the Palestinians, and expansion of the Israeli settlements. A year after the war in Iraq was launched, the plan to create a Palestinian state by 2005 had been scaled down to U.S. endorsement of Prime Minister Sharon's April 2004 proposal for unilateral Israeli disengagement from Gaza. President Bush enthusiastically endorsed it as offering "the Palestinians a chance to create a reformed, just and free government," no longer mentioning any deadline for a Palestinian state.

Bush's green light meant that until this state was created the Israelis would be free to create more "accomplished facts" that would determine the nature of any eventual settlement. The unilateral construction of a massive wall along the entire length of the Israeli–Palestinian frontier, placed primarily on the Palestinian side of the 1967 lines, was to be one of the central facts. By acquiescing to that and to continued settlement expansion, the United States abdicated any genuinely mediating role in a conflict that, together with the war in Iraq, continues to shape the political attitude of the region's increasingly activated population toward the United States.

Under Bush, U.S. policy toward the Middle East as a whole thus became strategically self-defeating. It not only ignored the fact that, left to themselves, the Israelis and the Palestinians could never resolve their differences on their own; it also ignored the fact that Israel, no matter how much more militarily powerful than its neighbors, could never impose a durable settlement by force alone. Such a settlement would lack acceptance, breed resentment, and provoke periodic violence. And as it did so, American interests in the region would continue to erode.

The transformation of the United States from a mediator between Israelis and Arabs into a partisan for Israel had the paradoxical effect of reducing U.S. ability to either decisively influence events (i.e., achieve peace) or enhance Israel's long-term security. On the contrary, the United States was simply being drawn more deeply into a region that was growing increasingly radicalized, and whose radicalization was revealing the limits of U.S. military power. Israel, meanwhile, was encouraged to persist in continuing construction of settlements at a time when its reliance on force was increasing the number of Arabs willing to die in a prolonged historic conflict with it.

By 2006 it should have been clear even to the Bush administration that neither the United States nor Israel, alone or together, has the power to crush and reorder the Middle East to its complete liking. The region is too large, its people less and less intimidated and more and more outraged with hatred, anger, and desperation. Increasing numbers are willing to engage in focused resistance or mindless terror. The more the United States and Israel react by expanding the scope and level of counterviolence, the more they will be drawn into a protracted and expanding war.

This misguided U.S. posture carries two long-range dangers: that the United States will eventually lose all its Arab friends and thus the capacity to influence their attitudes, with the consequence that for all intents and purposes the United States will be politically expelled from the Middle East; and that Israel will become involved in prolonged asymmetrical warfare, negating its technological military advantage, with the consequence that Israel will eventually be at mortal risk.

Moreover, given the American domestic political realities, these risks generate pressures for a widened U.S. military involvement in the region in order to check ever more distant threats to Israel. During the 1990s, prescriptive congressional legislation imposed an embargo on American dealings with Iran. Under Bush, antagonism toward Iran was elevated to a higher level, with the country proclaimed a charter member of the "axis of evil," the leading state sponsor of terrorism, and a potentially mortal threat not only to Israel (despite Israel's secret nuclear arsenal) but even to the United States (armed with tens of thousands of nuclear weapons and an array of delivery systems).

The resulting self-imposed prohibition on serious dealings with Tehran prompted the firm U.S. rebuff of an Iranian probe in 2003, shortly after the fall of Baghdad, regarding the possibility of a broad dialogue embracing both security and economic issues, including the problem of nuclear safeguards and even a two-state solution for the Israeli–Palestinian conflict. This probe was preceded in late 2001 by surprisingly helpful Iranian efforts to consolidate the government in Afghanistan after the United States removed the Taliban regime from power.

The net effect of a policy (or rather a stance) based on ostracism was to strengthen the fundamentalist elements in the Iranian regime while Iran proceeded steadily and stealthily to pursue a nuclear program that was at best ambiguous. While the Iranians have fervently declared that their goal is not the acquisition of nuclear weapons, it is a fact that the program's substantial progress over the past decade or so is gaining for Iran the capability to acquire such weapons. Bush's rhetorical condemnations and attempts at isolating Iran did little to clarify this situation or establish the basis for effectively addressing it.

In late spring of 2006, the United States was finally made to alter its position by two extraneous factors: the realization that the costly war in Iraq made the use of force against Iran a less attractive option, and a rising awareness of the futile, largely solitary U.S. attempts under Clinton and Bush to cope with the similar nuclear dilemma posed by North Korea. In the latter case, by early 2004 the United States found itself compelled by regional pressures to change its stance significantly.

Neither China nor Russia was prepared to follow America in a severe international ostracism of North Korea. It thus became clear that only a regional multilateral effort to induce North Korean self-restraint stood any chance of achieving an acceptable outcome. The Six-Party Talks, which formally commenced in 2004—involving the United States, the People's Republic of China, Japan, the Russian Federation, South Korea, and North Korea—were a far-reaching acknowledgment that the security of the Far East required some form of international architecture.

The same logic, accepted much more reluctantly by the Bush White House, finally prevailed with regard to Iran. The decision to explore negotiations with Iran was viewed as a betrayal by the administration's neocon zealots, who had hoped for direct U.S. military action, either to eliminate the key Iranian nuclear facilities or even to effect "regime change." Military limitations (the debilitating impact on U.S. armed forces of the Iraqi misadventure) and political considerations—strong opposition by the European Union and Russia to America's use of force—prompted the decision to explore the possibility of serious negotiations based on both inducements and sanctions. Nonetheless, continued instability in the Middle East meant that the more militant option might always be ignited by some future crisis. A sudden collision between Israel and Iran or simply Iranian recalcitrance and gross miscalculation could revive the clamor for a unilateral U.S. response.

But the issue of Iran demonstrated that even the Bush administration could not indefinitely escape the need for reality-based policy. Five years of "creating other new realities" had proven to be much more expensive, both internationally and domestically, than the president or his advisers could have expected. The administration's painful situation in Iraq inevitably created pressures for adjustment, for restoration of transatlantic comity and closer strategic collusion. Spurred by the active support for exploring some accommodation with Tehran from not only Great Britain, Germany, and France, but also Russia and China, the Iranian issue thus acted as a catalyst for a potentially significant, if reluctant, strategic adjustment.

"Reality-based" adjustments became also necessary in U.S. relations with Russia and China. Though in October 2004 Bush's then national security adviser self-servingly claimed, in an interview with a leading U.S. newspaper, that under Bush the United States had achieved "the best relationship that any administration has had with Russia" and also "the best relationship that any administration has had with China," in neither case was the relationship as close as in the recent past. Moreover, the strategic relationship between Russia and China was becoming closer than either country's relationship with the United States.

U.S.–Russian relations got off to a curious start shortly after Bush's first inaugural. In mid-2001 the new president undertook a trip to Europe, in the course of which he held a brief meeting in the capital of Slovenia with Russia's also relatively new president, Vladimir Putin, a former KGB colonel. The meeting lasted ninety minutes. With half of that time consumed by official translations, this meant that each side spoke for a little over twenty minutes. After the meeting, the president informed the astounded world press that "I have looked the man in the eye. I was able to get a sense of his soul." In brief, what mattered was not history, geopolitics, or shared values, but the pursuit of a personal relationship much like the earlier one between Clinton and Yeltsin.

The next several years saw Russia in steady retreat from the great chaotic leap toward democracy it had taken in the early 1990s. While this political regression was consistent with Putin's publicly stated view that "the collapse of the Soviet Union was the greatest geopolitical catastrophe of the century," Putin's authoritarian restoration did not alter Bush's assessment of him. Receiving him at Camp David in 2003, Bush hailed the Russian leader's "vision for Russia: a country at peace with its borders, with its neighbors and with the world, a country in which democracy and freedom and rule of law thrive." This was some four years after Putin had begun the ruthless oppression of the Chechens, costing by then about 200,000 Chechen lives.

That Russia had to be increasingly included in consultations regarding the Middle East, drawn into a constructive relationship with NATO, eventually allowed to join the WTO, and even included in the G7 (which thus became the G8) made practical sense (i.e., "reality-based" policy). It is more difficult to justify a policy based on an evaluation of the leader's soul if that evaluation leads one to overlook Russia's increasing attempts to impose its will on several newly independent states of the former Soviet Union (notably Ukraine, Georgia, and Moldova) and its sponsorship of the last dictatorial autocracy in Europe, Belarus.

Of still graver concern should be the growing strategic closeness of Russia and China, which neither Bush nor Secretary Rice seem to have noticed. After Bush's accession to power, the American relationship with China unfolded in a somewhat rocky fashion. An incident involving a collision between a U.S. intelligence aircraft, cruising near China's coasts, and an intercepting Chinese fighter plane created a brief burst of tension. After a forced landing by the damaged U.S. aircraft (the Chinese jet plunged into the sea, killing its pilot), the American crew was briefly detained while the two governments exchanged charges and countercharges. The incident, however, was contained, the crew released, and the matter soon resolved, though the United States was pressed into a one-sided apology.

Following this sour beginning, the relatively normal relationship that the Clinton administration had sustained was further tested by neoconservative initiatives to upgrade America's informal but deep ties with Taiwan. The Defense Department was especially active, with its deputy secretary stressing the need not only to upgrade Taiwan's defense capabilities but also engage in an almost formal dialogue with Taiwanese defense officials regarding security in China's immediate vicinity. (This contravened Beijing's view of Taiwan as part of "one China," a view acknowledged by earlier Republican and Democratic administrations.) Matters were not helped by the intensifying efforts of Taiwanese officials, abetted by their U.S. sympathizers both inside and outside the administration, to move toward official independence from the mainland.

The clock, however, could not be turned back, and the despised "reality" again dictated the need for accommodation. Eventually presidential visits were exchanged. Rapidly expanding American economic links with China and China's growing role in East Asia and in the global economy prompted the administration, in late 2001, to welcome China into the WTO. China soon became the key player in the Six-Party Talks with North Korea, further demonstrating its emergence as one of the world's major powers. Before long, China also became a key participant in the ongoing discussions among the United States, United Kingdom, France, Germany, and Russia regarding the risks posed by Iran's nuclear program.

Still, the Bush administration's success in sustaining the American–Chinese relationship should not obscure the fact that by the midpoint of Bush's presidency Chinese and Russian foreign policies on most pressing issues were closer to each other than either was to American policies. Regarding North Korea, Iran, the Middle East, and Central Asia as a whole, Chinese and Russian interests had become more compatible. Both regimes viewed America's militant promotion of electoral democracy with distaste. Each saw in this development an obvious threat to its own political stability. Also, Vladimir Putin and Hu Jintao projected a sense of personal kinship rooted in similarly cold but efficient styles of bureaucratic governance.

It may be worth noting that in the case of China, lingering historical resentments may have been reinforced by personal sensitivities, precipitated by the Bush administration's bizarrely inept handling of President Hu's visit to Washington in the late spring of 2006. The White House refused to hold a state dinner for him; at the arrival ceremony in the White House, the Chinese national anthem was announced as the anthem of the

Republic of China (the name used by Taiwan); Hu's official response to the public welcome was interrupted by a heckler whom White House security forces took their time in removing; loud protests were permitted late into the night outside Blair House, where Hu was staying; and an informal dinner for him in the city did not include the traditional playing of the national anthems or the trooping of the colors. With "face" being of special importance in Chinese culture, these slights were not helpful.

In any case, China's rising importance and Russia's recovery were creating a new geopolitical power alignment, not overtly directed at the United States like the old Sino-Soviet alliance, but driven by congruous regional interests as well as a shared (but not openly proclaimed) desire to clip America's overstretched wings. The Chinese quietly promoted a China-led Asian cooperative community in which the United States would at best play a secondary role, and China and Russia colluded to reduce the military presence in Central Asia that America had developed with its post–9/11 invasion of Afghanistan. Chinese political and economic influence was also being felt in the Middle East and Africa, as well as in the evolving economic relationship between China and Brazil.

Russia, meanwhile, was expanding its political and military ties with Venezuela while seeking to reduce America's influence within the former Soviet space. Europe's increased dependency on Russian energy sources also posed a risk to Atlantic solidarity. For example, the North European–Baltic pipeline project between Russia and Germany heightened Lithuanian and Polish fears of increased vulnerability to Russian energy blackmail.

American ability to mobilize Chinese and Russian support in the long-standing effort to impose limits on the North Korean and Iranian nuclear programs was also undermined by the unilateral decision of the Bush administration—motivated largely by its desire to forge an anti-Islamic terror coalition—to abruptly abandon its earlier opposition to India's nuclear weapons program. Remarkably, the United States reached that agreement with India without India's acceding the NPT requirement, which the five nuclear powers recognized by the treaty (America, Russia, Britain, China, and France) have accepted: to sign the treaty banning all nuclear tests and halt the production of plutonium and highly enriched uranium for weapons purposes. (China does not formally accept the second of these requirements.)

The decision to forge a U.S.–Indian strategic partnership, with provisions facilitating India's ability to expand its nuclear weapons arsenal, had to be especially troubling to China, which hitherto had maintained a posture of minimum strategic deterrence. A significant increase in India's nuclear arsenal could only increase the pressure on Beijing to abandon its strategic self-restraint. The U.S. action also undoubtedly lessened Beijing's inclination to do America's bidding with regard to North Korea and Iran.

America's selective and high-handed treatment of the nuclear issue is likely to intensify Chinese efforts to realign the overall structure of the international system. As its influence grows, China will increasingly see itself as a major global player that will not be bound by rules of the game invented largely in an era of American supremacy. While asserting a policy of peace, China has become more outspoken about its intention to redefine prevailing international arrangements. In the words of a leading Chinese journal on foreign affairs, China should "take the initiative and actively take part in the reform and restructuring of the international system so that it can better reflect the interests and demands of China. Otherwise, it will either exclude itself from the international system or be controlled by others or be forced to challenge the fait accompli system."

In cautiously but persistently seeking to enhance its international role, Beijing, looking beyond East Asia, is likely to target the Middle East next. To become a major presence there, China will stress that it can be a reliable customer for oil, a competitive supplier of manufactured goods as well as weaponry, and a politically friendly partner. Unlike the United States in recent years, China will neither disparage authoritarian rulers nor adopt a patronizing attitude toward other people's religious and cultural habits. The Arabs are unlikely to hear from Beijing the mentoring tones that have become the trademark of the Bush administration's foreign policy pronouncements. It is hardly far-fetched to imagine China becoming the dominant influence in the region if post–9/11 U.S. policies toward the region are not reassessed.

America's long-term interests also have been hurt by the lack of U.S. leadership on issues pertaining to the global commonweal. From 2001 to 2006, the unfolding human tragedy in Darfur was largely treated with indifference by the United States. The U.S. not only dismissed the International Criminal Court as a threat to its sovereignty but used its political leverage to obtain from friendly countries special legal exemptions for U.S. military personnel. The Kyoto Protocol became a whipping boy for White House skeptics of the global warming phenomenon, though much of the American public seems to share the administration's aversion to this subject. In an international poll among those who have heard about global warming, only 19 percent of American respondents said they gave the issue much thought, in contrast to 46 percent in France, 66 percent in Japan, 65 percent in India, and 34 percent in Russia. With public indifference abetted by official skepticism, it is no wonder that a comprehensive comparative study by Yale and Columbia Universities, released early in 2006 by the World Economic Forum, placed the United States behind most advanced countries in meeting critical environmental goals.

During the Bush presidency, negotiations in the continuing Doha Round of the WTO were stalemated by contending American and European views regarding agricultural subsidies, impeding wider global accommodation on trade issues that the poorer agriculture-dependent countries desperately need. Back in 2001, the world's richer countries promised that Doha would be "a development round" explicitly aimed at correcting the iniquities of the past and creating new opportunities for poorer countries. With a dearth of American leadership and the U.S.–European Union squabbling over agricultural liberalization, the promise has turned out to be like the horizon: a line that recedes as one moves toward it. (Both the United States and the European Union, as well as Japan, hugely subsidize their farmers: in 2005 the U.S. to the tune of $43 billion, Japan $47 billion, and the EU $134 billion.) Moreover, narrow self-interest made the Americans and Europeans indifferent to the vulnerability of poorer countries' nascent manufacturing industries to competition from more advanced economies.

Last but not least, the United States has been derelict in fulfilling the commitment it undertook in Monterrey in 2002 to "make concrete efforts" to increase substantially the level of its official development aid. At the same time, the United States has kept a tight grip on the World Bank, on the grounds that it is its largest donor, and the U.S. has also been reticent regarding the U.N. Millennium Development goals for the reduction of global poverty, hunger, and disease. Despite official rhetoric about "compassion," on a per capita basis the United States remains one of the least generous contributors to development aid for the world's most impoverished countries. (It is small consolation that oil-rich Russia is even worse. China, on the other hand, is improving its performance.)

Given this record, it is no wonder that global alienation from America and worldwide doubts about Bush's leadership have steadily risen. One especially ominous development is occurring close to home: the increasing linkage in Latin America between the rise of democracy and the rise in anti-American sentiments. In the past, the more intense manifestations of anti-American popular feeling were confined to Castro-type communist or Peronist-type nationalist regimes. Recently, however, mass political activism in Latin America has taken the form of populist democracy, with the United States as a target of social, economic, and political grievances. The two most populous states in Latin America have already become outspoken in their resentment of U.S. policies: Brazil over the stalemate in the Doha Round, and Mexico over U.S. immigration policies and the double-edged consequences of

NAFTA, especially for Mexican agriculture. Before long, the populist contagion may spread to Central America and the Caribbean states as well.

These negative international tendencies are compounded by the alarmist tone of the Bush administration's domestic response to the new global challenge of terrorism. It has chosen to propagate an atmosphere of national fear in the face of an inherently unclear and unpredictable threat. Past U.S. presidents, in times of national peril, strove to project calm determination and inspire public confidence. That was the case after Pearl Harbor, as well as during the worst days of the Cold War, when a nuclear war (either deliberately initiated or caused by a technological misfire) could have killed more than 150 million people in a few hours.

The near-term threat of terrorism does not remotely approach that level. Yet when confronted by the possibility of painful but essentially sporadic acts of terrorism, Bush made it a point to designate himself a "wartime" president. Official stoking of public anxiety spawned a huge array of terror "experts" conjuring apocalyptic predictions. The mass media plunged into a competition in popularizing almost on a daily basis their various horror scenarios. As a result a confident national psyche is being transformed into a nation driven by fear. In its present garrison-state mentality, America risks becoming a huge gated community, self-isolated from the world. The nation's tradition of civil rights and its capacity to project itself worldwide as an appealing and self-confident democracy are diminished.

As Global Leader III, George W. Bush misunderstood the historical moment, and in just five years dangerously undermined America's geopolitical position. In seeking to pursue a policy based on the delusion that "we are an empire now, and when we act, we create our own reality," Bush endangered America. Europe is now increasingly alienated. Russia and China are both more assertive and more in step. Asia is turning away and organizing itself while Japan is quietly considering how to make itself more secure. Latin American democracy is becoming populist and anti-American. The Middle East is fragmenting and on the brink of explosion. The world of Islam is inflamed by rising religious passion and anti-imperialist nationalisms. Throughout the world, public opinion polls show that U.S. policy is widely feared and even despised.

It follows that the next U.S. president will have to mount a monumental effort to restore America's legitimacy as the major guarantor of global security and reidentify America with a common response to intensifying social dilemmas in a world that is now politically awakened and not susceptible to imperial domination. Arnold Toynbee, in his classic study of history, ascribed the fall of empires ultimately to "suicidal statecraft" by their leaders. The saving grace for America may be that, unlike emperors, U.S. presidents, including catastrophic ones, are limited to eight years in office.

6

Beyond 2008

(and America's Second Chance)

E ACH OF THE THREE GLOBAL LEADERS DEFINED
his own historical essence: Bush I was the policeman, re-
lying on power and legitimacy to preserve traditional stability;
Clinton was the social welfare advocate, counting on globalization to generate progress; Bush II was the vigilante, mobilizing domestic fears to pursue a self-declared existential
struggle against the forces of evil.

Each president thus tapped, in a different way, the instincts of the American people, whose reactions magnified
each leader's strengths and weaknesses. Each could act effectively as a global leader only if his sense of the historical moment coincided with the gut feelings of the American people,
and if (though this is inherently difficult to determine) his
view of the global challenge coincided with the spirit and
character of worldwide political and social change. The appraisal that follows is therefore an indirect assessment of

America's capacity to sustain effective, responsible global leadership over the long term.

Writing about America's world role more than three decades ago, the distinguished French political theorist and historian Raymond Aron argued in his monumental book *The Imperial Republic* that

> The national interest of the United States. . . will not win over any state or arouse any sentiment of loyalty unless it appears jointly liable for an international order, an order of power as well as law. . . It is legitimate to regret the passing of the ages in which dispassionate and amoral diplomacy was merely a subtle exercise in influences and statecraft. In the twentieth century *the strength of a great power is diminished if it ceases to serve an idea.* (Italics added)

The last sentence is critical. The exercise of global leadership today requires an instinctive grasp of the spirit of the times in a world that is stirring, interactive, and motivated by a vague but pervasive sense of prevailing injustice in the human condition. The rising intensity of aroused political emotions can either be channeled in constructive directions or harnessed by demagogues and fanatics in a global wildfire of conflicts. In the post–Cold War era, America can be the decisive factor determining which of the two will prevail. Hence it is time for an appraisal of how well superpower America has done on the world scene since 1990 under the direction of the first three global leaders.

How Has America Led?

In a word, badly. Though in some dimensions, such as the military, American power may be greater in 2006 than in 1991, the country's capacity to mobilize, inspire, point in a shared direction and thus shape global realities has significantly declined. Fifteen years after its coronation as global leader, America is becoming a fearful and lonely democracy in a politically antagonistic world.

MAJOR GEOPOLITICAL TRENDS ADVERSE TO THE UNITED STATES, 2006

Intensifying hostility to the West throughout the world of Islam

An explosive Middle East

An Iran predominant in the Persian Gulf

A volatile, nuclear-armed Pakistan

A disaffected Europe

A resentful Russia

China setting up an East Asian community

Japan more isolated in Asia

Populist anti-U.S. wave in Latin America

Breakdown of the nonproliferation regime

Looking back, America's overall performance in the three central missions of its global leadership fell short of what was attainable. Insecurity has become more pervasive even though the total number of ongoing conflicts worldwide has actually dropped since the end of the Cold War. Nuclear capability has spread to four additional countries, two overtly and two ambiguously. Progress on human welfare issues has been sporadic and environmental concerns have not gained high priority. Partly as a result of these failures, American leadership has lost much of its legitimacy, the worldwide credibility of the American presidency has been undermined, and the moral standing of America has been tarnished.

Had world public opinion been given the opportunity in the early 1990s to designate a single state as the most desirable steward of global security, a large majority would have chosen America. In 2006 that would certainly not be the case. The blame for this rests on the shoulders of the three presidents who led the first global superpower, but not evenly. The first did not seize the opportunity offered to America, the second was too complacent in addressing it, and the third turned his opportunity into a self-inflicted and festering wound while precipitating rising global hostility toward America.

Bush I admittedly did well in responding to the collapse of the Soviet Union, a dangerous process that he handled with delicacy and skill. The original sin of his administration, however, is rooted in the failure to give any serious substance to its often-invoked "new world order" slogan at a time when the entire world system was not only malleable but highly responsive to America's political and moral leadership.

Paradoxically, that failure was related to the domain in which Bush I did excel: power politics. He let his major success—expelling Saddam Hussein from Kuwait in 1991 with impressive military effectiveness and backed by a skillfully contrived political coalition that included Arab states—become strategically inconclusive. This victory should have been exploited to achieve a breakthrough in the Middle Eastern stalemate. Instead, Israeli–Palestinian hostilities were allowed to simmer, and unresolved conflicts were bequeathed to Bush's successors, even though the region at that moment was susceptible to a decisive diplomatic initiative backed by America's recent successful use of power. Iraq was left to fester. Saddam's defeat was not exploited to initiate a dialogue with Iran. Afghanistan, just freed from the Soviet invasion, was largely ignored. Anti-Americanism in the region continued to spread.

Clinton, initially less interested in world affairs, replaced the new world order with the concept of "irreversible" globalization. But its alleged inevitability conveniently absolved the new global leader of the obligation to formulate and pursue any deliberate strategy. Nonetheless, he did bite the bullet on two vital geopolitical issues. After prolonged hesitation, in his second term he moved forward with enlarging NATO, paving the way for the subsequent EU enlargement, and he eventually mobilized a collective military response to the brutal ethnic cleansing in the Balkans.

But lacking a more vigorous strategic determination, he was susceptible to an "enemy du jour" vacillation abetted by various pressure groups, and he gave the Middle East only occasional attention. His response to each of the three smoldering situations in the region was heavily influenced by domestic pressures: the Iran problem was artificially linked to Libya by congressional legislation, Iraq was left to drift, and the unresolved Israeli–Palestinian conflict was allowed to stalemate after the assassination of Prime Minister Rabin.

The death of Rabin signaled a turn to the right in Israel that eventually led to an alliance with the mushrooming neoconservative pressure group and the Christian right in the United States. In the process, the U.S. stance—again in large part under domestic stimuli, especially from the Israel lobby—shifted from that of an impartial mediator to proponent of the Israeli preference to delay any final settlement. As a consequence, America's capacity to mediate diminished substantially.

Clinton inherited an America without a global rival, but he did not exploit his opportunities to create a wider framework of accommodation that might have averted some looming dangers. Proliferation was not tackled with determination. A serious effort to address global social problems would have recognized the need for the American people to accept some measure of restraint, but the president's own inclinations were hardly conducive to such a change in the national mood. The country was hardly aware of deepening resentment around the world and the growing restlessness it reflected.

Under Bush II, foreign policy was largely dormant for six months before being galvanized by the terrorist attack of 9/11. The world rallied around America, presenting Washington with a unique opportunity to forge a global coalition. Alas, the foreign policy that the president forged became outspokenly unilateralist ("if you are not with us, you are against us"),

FIGURE 6 ❖ GLOBAL LEADERSHIP:
A PRESIDENTIAL REPORT CARD

	Bush I	Clinton	Bush II
Atlantic Alliance	A	A	D
Post-Soviet Space	B	B–	B–
Far East	C+	B–	C+
Middle East	B–	D	F
Proliferation	B	D	D
Peacekeeping	n.a.	B+	C
Environment	C	B-	F
Global Trade/Poverty	B–	A–	C–
Overall	**Solid: B**	**Uneven: C**	**Failed: F**
Comment	Tactical skill but missed strategic opportunities	Major gap between potential and performance	A simplistic dogmatic worldview prompts self-destructive unilateralism

demagogic, fear-driven as well as fear-inspiring, and politically exploitative of the slogan "we are a nation at war." It ultimately plunged America into a solitary war of choice in Iraq.

Because of Bush's self-righteously unilateral conduct of U.S. foreign policy after 9/11, the evocative symbol of America in the eyes of much of the world ceased to be the Statue of Liberty and instead became the Guantanamo prison camp. America justified its war in Iraq by demagogy buttressed by dubious factual allegations and pursued it with costly self-delusions, intensifying the region's many conflicts even while proclaiming that it was giving birth to a new and more democratic Middle East. American public opinion, at first solidly behind the president's militant rhetoric, split into opposing but also largely confused perspectives. Historical anxiety became more pervasive.

At this point, it is fair to ask what might have been. Might the world be very different if the three global leaders had acted differently? Though history cannot be rewound like a tape recorder, there is some merit in enlightened counterfactual speculation. It can even provide a partial guide to the future.

The case could be made that since the end of the Cold War U.S. policy missed two grand historical opportunities. The first, in which blame has to be shared with others, was the failure to capitalize on the post–Cold War victory to shape—even in some fashion to institutionalize—an Atlantic community with a shared strategic global focus. There were moments after 1991 when the two sides of the Atlantic were engaged in common enterprises: during the first Gulf War, during the NATO interventions in Bosnia and Kosovo, and in Afghanistan after 9/11. In these instances, collaboration was intentionally fostered and proved successful.

The expansion of NATO and the European Union created an optimistic historical perspective that could have been galvanized more purposefully to create a transatlantic decision-making process focused on peacekeeping and nonproliferation. The habit of shaping policies together and sharing the burden of their implementation might thereby have been fostered.

Much the same could be said regarding the long-term interest of America and Europe in jointly creating a global economic order that would be increasingly responsive to the legitimate demands of the developing nations for greater equity and opportunity.

America and Europe together could be the decisive force for good in the world. Separately, and especially if feuding, they guarantee stalemate and greater disorder. During the decade and a half of its preponderance, the United States regrettably did not make a concerted effort to engage the European Union in a common attempt to institutionalize global cooperation through more deliberate joint foreign policy planning and decision making. Furthermore, some U.S. reactions to the emergence of a larger and more confident Europe indicated uneasiness and even fear that a Europe led jointly by Germany and France might not be in America's interest. That concern prompted Washington to quietly encourage Great Britain to be more "Atlanticist" and less "European" (London was only too eager to accommodate).

Admittedly, Europeans would have needed American prodding to join in a genuine partnership. The momentum for political integration rapidly waned after the adoption of the euro and eventually even resulted in the rejection of the proposed European constitution. France felt reduced in its role as the prime mover of European unity by the emergence of a united and politically assertive Germany and so was tempted to play up the special Paris–Moscow relationship. Eventually it took the lead in rejecting the EU constitution that it had earlier promoted.

More deliberate U.S.–EU cooperation might have spilled over into other strategic domains. The effort to draw Russia

FIGURE 7 ❖ THE CENTRALITY OF THE
ATLANTIC COMMUNITY IN WORLD AFFAIRS

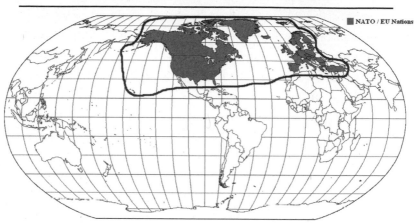

■ NATO / EU Nations

The economic and military strength of the Atlantic community makes it the gravitational center of world affairs. While only 13 percent of the world's people are in NATO and/or EU nations, together they account for 63 percent of the world's GDP, producing over $27 trillion worth of goods and services in 2005, and over 77 percent of global military spending, allocating over $780 billion to their militaries in 2005 alone.

Prepared by Brett Edkins

into a closer relationship with the Atlantic community might have been more successful if the United States and the European Union had made a joint endeavor to engage Russia while disabusing it of any imperial nostalgia regarding the newly independent states of the former Soviet Union. On both scores, the West's position was ambiguous and divided. Though Russia clearly was not ready to consider actual membership in either the European Union or NATO, it was never made to feel that it would be genuinely embraced in some special association with these key institutions. Worse still, the Western allies never made it clear to Moscow that it risked isolation if it chose to reestablish authoritarianism at home and engage in neoimperialist tactics toward Moldova, Ukraine, and Georgia, not to mention the tragic case of Chechnya. Instead, Russia was continuously flattered as a new democracy and its leaders personally propitiated.

A joint and truly cooperative transatlantic policy might also have resulted in an earlier and more effective response to the threat of nuclear proliferation, in the first instance from Iran but perhaps even from India and Pakistan. The sad fact is that the United States has been highly selective in its approach to nonproliferation, either supporting or winking at the acquisition of nuclear weapons by its friends. In mid-2006, an international commission sponsored by Sweden reported to the U.N. secretary general that efforts to prevent nuclear weapons proliferation had stalled largely due to a lack of U.S. leadership. It criticized Washington's attitude toward proliferation and warned that if America "does not take the lead, there could be more nuclear tests and new nuclear arms races."

Instead of taking the lead, the United States has tacitly favored India's nuclear weapons buildup while staunchly opposing Iran's. America's European allies favored negotiations with Iran but prevailed on Washington to explore that option only in 2006. A concerted transatlantic effort to solve the Middle East conflict might have also created the grounds for a Middle Eastern nuclear-free zone agreement, resolving the interlocking dilemmas posed by Israel's undeclared nuclear arsenal and the ambiguous intent of Iran's ongoing nuclear program.

A habit of genuine transatlantic consultation, deliberately fostered to enhance mutual confidence, might have also facilitated progress in the intractable north–south stalemate over the ground rules for globalization. The Doha Round of WTO talks stalled largely because of persisting American–European differences, which made it easier for such countries as Japan and China to protect their immediate interests to the disadvantage of the global commonweal. Greater flexibility by the Atlantic community would have exerted pressure on Japan (regarding agricultural subsidies) and China (currency devaluation and manufacturing exports) to be more equitable in the trade negotiations.

There is also a special security aspect to the Atlantic dimension of "what might have been." With Japan drawn more directly into transatlantic strategizing, there might have been less inclination both there and in the United States to focus on upgrading Japan's military capabilities to counter China's growing strength. That might have avoided rising pressures within the Chinese political elite, especially the military, to enhance the Sino–Russian security connection.

America's failure to move decisively on the Israeli–Palestinian problem during the fifteen years of its supremacy represents the second major "what if." Had there been such movement, and had it involved a joint effort to induce the two sides to accept an equitable compromise formula spelled out explicitly by the United States and the European Union, the Middle East might have avoided its subsequent degeneration into worsening violence, and a shared sense of strategic purpose and accomplishment would have been injected into transatlantic relations.

A decisive and successful transatlantic push during the 1990s for an Israeli–Palestinian settlement might have avoided the self-defeating U.S. military adventure in Iraq. Instead, the Israeli–Palestinian stalemate, followed by the unilateral U.S. invasion of Iraq, prompted an American-Europe split. Only those in a state of self-serving denial can argue that the persistent Israeli–Palestinian conflict has not been instrumental in igniting widespread Arab hostility toward America. The destabilizing effect of that hostility, intensified by the war in Iraq, poses the long-range risk of America's eventual expulsion from the region. Neither the region's ruling elites nor the Chinese are ignoring this prospect. The vulnerable Middle Eastern elites need a foreign protector, and China needs stable access to the oil those elites control. Each side has thus something to offer the other. That an arrangement inimical to U.S. interests might be looming should not be lightly dismissed.

Will America Have a Second Chance?

Certainly. In large measure that is so because no other power is capable of playing the role that America *potentially* can and should play. Europe still lacks the requisite political unity and will to be a global power. Russia cannot decide whether it wishes to be an authoritarian, imperialist, socially backward Eurasian state or a genuinely modern European democracy. China is emerging rapidly as the dominant Far Eastern mainland power, but it has a rival in Japan, and it is still unclear how China will resolve the basic contradiction between its freewheeling economic momentum and the bureaucratic centralism of its political system. India has yet to prove that it can sustain unity and democracy if its religious, ethnic, and linguistic diversity becomes politically charged.

America has a monopoly on global military reach, an economy second to none, and peerless technological innovation, all of which give it unique worldwide political clout. Moreover, there is a widespread, if unspoken, practical recognition that the international system needs an effective stabilizer, and that the most likely short-term alternative to a constructive American world role is chaos. An intelligent Global Leader IV should still be able to exploit that feeling to tap what's left of the reservoir of goodwill toward America. Though hostility toward the United States has risen to unprecedented levels and has not yet crested, an America aware of its responsibilities, measured in its presidential rhetoric, sensitive to the complexities of the human condition, and consensual rather than abrasive in its external relations (in brief, entirely different from its recent emanation) is an America that much of the world would still like to see at the global helm.

But make no mistake: it will take years of deliberate effort and genuine skill to restore America's political credibility and legitimacy. The next president should draw strategic lessons from America's recent mistakes as well as its past successes. To be sure, historical speculation cannot be the basis for specific policy recommendations given changed circumstances, unexpected events, and novel challenges. But counterfactual speculation—as summarized on the preceding pages—does help us define priorities and reminds us of fundamental realities. That applies particularly to the unfulfilled potential of the Atlantic community and the mounting costs of procrastination regarding peace in the Middle East.

America should draw additional lessons from its earlier achievements. During the long Cold War, Europe was the central political arena and the central stake. America prevailed because it pursued a policy notable for its wisdom and patience. That policy relied heavily on enduring alliances and policies that deliberately sought to unite America's friends and divide its enemies. America resolutely practiced a strategic doctrine of deterrence, and it did so despite the high levels of threat (especially once the Soviet Union achieved strategic parity with the United States) under which the Cold War had to be waged. Even though a nuclear war between the United States and the Soviet Union could at any moment have taken upwards of 150 million lives in just a few hours, American leaders did not propagate fear as a means of sustaining national determination (it's hard to imagine Eisenhower or Reagan proclaiming himself a "war president"), and they patiently balanced strategic firmness with diplomatic flexibility.

That policy differed substantially from the nation's stance, especially after 9/11, regarding the challenges emanating from the Middle East, the region that has become the new central arena and the new central stake for the American superpower. American policy has divided its friends while uniting its foes, fear has been exploited to mobilize public support for policy, and strategic impatience and self-ostracism have narrowed U.S. diplomatic options.

But beyond such specific policy issues, America's future acceptability as world leader depends on answers to large and complex questions regarding:

1. The nature of the American system itself: Is the American system structurally equipped to formulate and sustain a global policy that not only protects American interests but also promotes global security and well-being?

2. The American social model in a world of rising expectations: Is American society ready to sustain a global leadership role that calls for some degree of responsible self-restraint derived from a basic understanding of global trends?

3. The American grasp of the world's novel condition: Does the nation intuitively sense what the global political awakening implies for America's own future?

The Foreign Policy Process

The structural handicaps that infringe on America's capacity to formulate and sustain a long-term commitment to global leadership are partially rooted in the unique circumstances of America's birth as a nation. But they are also the result of systemic degeneration prompted by the impact of modern communications and money on American politics.

The American constitutional system, with its separation of powers, was an act of genius. It created an unsurpassed design for protecting individual freedom while providing for a cross-checking process of national decision making. This complex arrangement was sheltered by America's geographic isolation and the resulting absence of any proximate security threat. More than 250 years later, superpower America is now massively intertwined with the world and preponderant within it. Yet its leaders—sensitive to changing domestic moods but often slow to grasp changing global realities—are inclined to formulate policies of worldwide impact largely in response to domestic stimuli. That contributes to the widespread (and not unjustified) view around the world that parochial America projects its own pet preoccupations, latest slogans, and special interests onto the global arena. Worldwide skepticism about the U.S. announcement of a "war on terror" is but the latest reflection of this tendency.

The absence of any institutionalized mechanism engaging both the executive and the legislative branches in global planning compounds the problem. Neither the executive branch nor the legislative has any formal process for taking a long-range look at the global future and consulting about needed policies. The executive branch is notoriously weak in coordinated planning, and efforts to locate such planning in the National Security Council have resulted in long-term interests being subordinated to the short-term. The legislative branch focuses almost exclusively on immediate domestic concerns.

Moreover, the executive and legislative branches, jealous of their traditional prerogatives, do not collaborate to formulate a national grand strategy. The presidential State of the Union address could have evolved into a serious consultation with the Congress. Instead, it has become largely an annual spectacle of patriotic slogans, partisan gymnastics tabulated by the number of standing ovations, and the introduction of various "heroes" seated next to the First Lady. Congressional hearings are hardly better. Their central goal is to expose the recent failings, real or otherwise, of the executive branch.

A useful corrective would be to establish some regular executive–legislative consultative planning mechanism for foreign policy, supported by a combined staff. Since its central mission would be to do long-term planning and its central role would be to promote substantive consultations between the president and the congressional leadership, the result need not threaten the separation of powers. It would not supplant the president's executive prerogatives because it would not be a decision-making body. But a periodic in-depth joint global policy review with pertinent congressional leaders would help crystallize a more widely shared sense of direction.

Greater coherence in national policy also calls for correcting the widespread impression, not only at home but increasingly abroad, that some aspects of U.S. foreign policy are for sale. The growing role of foreign policy lobbies in Washington is both the cause of that perception and a reflection of it. Though lobbies representing large voting constituencies with strong foreign attachments have long been part of the legislative process, the nature of their influence, the focus of their efforts, and their composition have changed, compounding the structural handicaps of U.S. global policy making.

In the past, ethnic lobbies with a foreign policy interest tended to derive their influence from the voting loyalty of their allegedly numerous constituents. Whether it be the Irish–American lobby or the Polish–American lobby, U.S. politicians—especially presidential candidates—took their aroused feelings seriously. FDR, during sensitive World War II negotiations with Stalin over Poland's place in postwar Europe, at one point even explicitly justified his unwillingness to formally confirm the concessions he had orally promised to the Soviet dictator by arguing that doing so might anger Polish American voters on the eve of the 1944 presidential elections.

In more recent times, the capacity to raise and target electoral campaign funds has become a more important source of influence for foreign policy lobbies than their claimed voting strength. Increased congressional dependence on costly and almost permanent campaigning is the root cause of this trend. The high expense of TV campaigns has turned targeted funding support (or opposition) into a crucial instrument for gaining influence. This explains the growing role of highly motivated Israeli–American, Cuban–American, Greek–American, Armenian–American lobbies and others, all highly effective in mobilizing financial support for their particular causes.

Given the visible success of the foregoing, it is only a question of time before a Hindu–American, Chinese–American, or Russian–American lobby also deploys substantial resources to influence congressional legislation. (A Mexican–American lobby is also emerging, but it is more likely to capitalize in the traditional manner on the size of its electorate.) The Russian press, for example, has candidly speculated on the potential advantages for Russia of a well-oiled Russian–American foreign policy lobby, capable of hiring lobbying firms, sponsoring research institutes, and engaging in various other promotional activities designed to advance Russian interests.

The effectiveness of such lobbies is reflected in the growing prevalence of congressional legislation deliberately limiting the executive branch's foreign policy choices. Early examples were the 1974 arms embargo against Turkey, favored by the Greek lobby, and the Jackson-Vanik Act imposing trade restrictions on the Soviet Union unless Jewish emigration was liberalized. Recently this kind of legislation has grown more frequent. Examples from the preceding decade and a half include the passage (promoted by the Cuban, Israeli, Taiwanese, and Armenian foreign policy lobbies respectively) of the Cuban Democracy Act (1992) and the Helms-Burton Act (1996); the Iran-Iraq Arms Non-Proliferation Act (1992), the Iran-Libya Sanctions Act (1996), Syria Accountability Act (2003), and Palestine Anti-Terrorism Act (2006); the Taiwan Security Enhancement Act (2000); and Section 907 of the Freedom Support Act (1992), directed largely at Azerbaijan. The Christian lobby was instrumental in promoting the International Religious Freedom Act (1998).

This fragmentation of foreign policy making ill serves the American national interest. As Henry Kissinger noted in his recent book, *Does America Need a Foreign Policy?*, because of domestic pressure groups, "Congress not only legislates the tactics of foreign policy but also seeks to impose a code of conduct on other nations by a plethora of sanctions. Scores of nations now find themselves under such sanctions." In addition to a more systematic process of planning and consultation between the executive and legislative branches, stricter lobbying laws should be adopted imposing limits on the ability of foreign interests to sponsor and finance domestically based foreign policy lobbies. Moreover, the lobbies themselves should be subject to closer scrutiny and their financial influence to more detailed public accountability.

The American Social Model

In mutually compounding ways, material self-indulgence, persistent social shortcomings, and public ignorance about the world increase the difficulty the American democracy faces in formulating a globally appealing platform for effective world leadership. Americans must recognize that their patterns of consumption will soon collide head-on with increasingly impatient egalitarian aspirations. Whether through the exploitation of natural resources, excessive energy consumption, indifference to global ecology, or the exorbitant size of houses for the well-to-do, indulgent self-gratification at home conveys indifference to the persisting deprivations of much of the world. (Just try to imagine a world in which 2.5 billion Chinese and Indians consume as much energy per capita as Americans do.) That reality the American public has yet to assimilate.

To lead, America must not only be sensitive to global realities. It must also be socially attractive. That calls for a broader national consensus in favor of correcting the key failings of the American social model. Writing in *Out of Control* a decade or so ago, I listed twenty major shortcomings that inhibit America's ability to project a globally appealing example. Since then, nine of the fourteen categories that can be precisely measured actually show a regressive trend.* During this time, for instance, income inequality has risen to new heights, with the best paid rewarded at almost obscene levels while average wages have barely crept upward.

---

*For example, over the past decade and a half, the U.S. national debt has increased in both absolute totals and percentage of GDP; the trade deficit has grown exponentially; net savings have decreased significantly in both absolute terms and percentage of GDP; the percentage of under sixty-five-year-olds without health insurance has increased; the percentage share of income for the rich has increased; tort costs have almost doubled; the percentage of African Americans living in poverty has increased, as has the percentage of Americans reporting illicit drug use; upward social mobility for the poor has declined.

The needed social reassessment cannot come quickly because habits and expectations are deeply engrained. But it can be encouraged by deliberate civic education that stresses the notion of service to a higher cause than oneself. As some have occasionally urged, a major step in that direction would be the adoption of an obligatory period of national service for every young adult, perhaps involving a variety of congressionally approved domestic or foreign good works. Currently the only obligatory civic duty for all Americans is to pay taxes (with loopholes for major corporations and the rich). Even participation in national defense, except in dire national emergency, is a voluntary act made financially attractive to the less privileged.

A period of national service dedicated to the global commonweal would help instill a civic consciousness that is essential if America is to sustain an intelligent, compassionate global leadership. It would appeal to the idealistic instincts of the young and give them the experience of working for a larger and selfless goal, and it would help stimulate public awareness of longer-range domestic or global social choices that America needs to make.

Given that America is a genuine democracy, its ability to pursue a constructive global policy has to be derived ultimately from a well-informed public. Yet the citizens of the world's only superpower, which ultimately makes its decisions on the basis of the popular will, are abysmally ignorant about the world. The vast majority of the American people have little knowledge of world history or geography. Neither print nor television news offers much by way of corrective, and public education is particularly weak in the two disciplines mentioned above.

Only about 1 percent of American college students study abroad, and most have not even the vaguest sense of where other nations are. A study by the National Geographic Society in 2002 found that 85 percent of young Americans could not locate Iraq or Afghanistan on the map, 60 percent could not find Great Britain, and 29 percent could not even point out the Pacific Ocean. Moreover, few Americans currently study the languages that are likely to be internationally important in the future, such as Chinese or Arabic. Public ignorance, easily reinforced by fear, creates unfavorable conditions for any serious discussion of what America needs to do in order to play a constructive role in the world.

In the years to come, the president must exert personal leadership in the requisite public education. The president needs to speak more often of America's global responsibility and define it in a manner that does not intensify public anxiety but focuses attention on problem solving. Perhaps an annual presidential speech on the state of the world would be a useful step, precipitating public commentaries, op-eds, and (one hopes) a greater awareness not only that America affects the world but that the world also affects America in ways hitherto unimaginable.

The Global Political Awakening

America's most difficult task, but historically the most critical, will be to embody to the world at large an idea whose time has come. Twice in its history the nation has done so, with universally positive effect. In 1776 America defined the meaning of freedom for a world just beginning to seek it. In the twentieth century, America became the principal defender of democracy against totalitarianism. In today's restless world, America needs to identify itself with the quest for universal human dignity, a dignity that embodies both freedom and democracy but also implies respect for cultural diversity and recognizes that persisting injustices in the human condition must be remedied.

The worldwide yearning for human dignity is the central challenge inherent in the phenomenon of global political awakening. As I have argued elsewhere (*The American Interest*), that awakening is socially massive, politically radicalizing, and geographically universal. Though the global scope of today's political awakening is novel, the phenomenon itself has a history beginning with the French Revolution of 1789, which generated, first in France and then throughout Europe, a contagious populist activism of unprecedented intensity and social scope. An aroused mass political consciousness was stimulated by the spread of literacy—notably pamphleteering—and the country was galvanized by populist rallies, manifestos, and flaming rhetoric on the public squares of urban centers, in numerous political clubs, and even in remote villages. That burst of activism engaged not only the new bourgeoisie and the new urban lower classes (the *sans culottes*) but also the peasants, clergy, and aristocrats.

During the subsequent centuries, political awakening has spread gradually but inexorably. The liberal European revolutions of 1848, and more generally the nationalist movements of the late nineteenth and early twentieth centuries, reflected the new populist passions and growing mass commitment. The same political awakening precipitated several decades of civil conflict in China, with the Boxer Rebellion at the start of the twentieth century leading to a nationalist revolution culminating at midcentury with the communist victory. Anticolonial sentiments galvanized India, where the tactic of passive resistance effectively disarmed imperial domination. After World War II, anticolonial political stirrings elsewhere ended the remaining European empires.

In the twenty-first century the population of much of the developing world is now politically stirring. It is a population conscious of social injustice to an unprecedented degree and resentful of its deprivations and lack of personal dignity. Nearly universal access to radio, television, and the Internet is creating a community of shared resentments and envy that transcends sovereign borders and poses a challenge to both existing states and the global hierarchy, on top of which America still perches.

Attempts to analyze the future of China or India must consider the likely behavior of populations whose social and political aspirations are shaped by impulses that are no longer exclusively local in origin. The same applies to the Middle East, Southeast Asia, and North Africa, as well as to the Indian populations of Latin America, who increasingly define their aspirations in reaction to the outside world's allegedly hostile impact on them. Many, disliking the status quo, are susceptible to being mobilized against those whom they perceive as self-interestedly preserving it.

Third World youth are particularly volatile. The rapidly expanding demographic bulge in the twenty-five and under age bracket represents a huge mass of impatience. This group's revolutionary spearhead is likely to emerge from among the millions of students concentrated in the often intellectually dubious tertiary-level educational institutions of developing countries. Semimobilized in large congregations and connected by the Internet, they are positioned to replay, on a far vaster scale, what occurred years earlier in Mexico City and Tiananmen Square. Revolutionaries-in-waiting, they represent the equivalent of the militant proletariat of the nineteenth and twentieth centuries.

To sum up, the political awakening is now global in geographic scope, comprehensive in social scale (with only remote peasant communities still politically passive), strikingly youthful in demographic profile and thus receptive to rapid political mobilization, and transnational in sources of inspiration because of the cumulative impact of literacy and mass communications. As a result, modern populist political passions can be aroused even against a distant target, despite the absence of a unifying doctrine such as Marxism.

Only by identifying itself with the idea of universal human dignity—with its basic requirement of respect for culturally diverse political, social, and religious emanations—can America overcome the risk that the global political awakening will turn against it. Human dignity encompasses freedom and democracy but goes beyond them. It involves social justice, gender equality, and, above all, respect for the world's cultural and religious mosaic. That is yet another reason why impatient democratization, imposed from outside, is doomed to fail. Stable liberal democracy has to be nurtured by stages and fostered from within.

The Geopolitics of Global Political Awakening

Global political awakening is historically anti-imperial, politically anti-Western, and emotionally increasingly anti-American. In the process, it is setting in motion a major shift in the global center of gravity. That in turn is altering the global distribution of power, with major implications for America's role in the world.

The foremost geopolitical effect of global political awakening is the demise of the imperial age. Empires have existed throughout history, and in recent times American paramountcy has often been described as a new global empire. This is somewhat of a misnomer, implying basic continuity with previous imperial systems, but some similarity is undeniable, and that makes America the focus of anti-imperial sentiment.

Imperial stability has historically depended on skilled domination, superior military organization, and—ultimately most important—political passivity on the part of dominated peoples against their less numerous but more assertive dominators. (The British at one point controlled India with only four thousand civil servants and officers.) Initially empires evolved by territorial expansion to adjoining areas, a pattern followed in more modern times by the Russian (then Soviet) empire. The more recent Western European empires grew predominantly through superior transoceanic navigational capabilities motivated by trade and greed for valuable minerals. Modern imperialism is thus largely a Western emanation.

That phenomenon reached its apogee by the end of the nineteenth century and was largely in retreat throughout the twentieth. While the immediate causes of that retreat were the two world wars, its underlying momentum came from the political awakening of the dominated peoples: nationalist agitation, a rising sense of separate political identity, and growing awareness of social deprivation, culminating in a view of foreign domination as an affront to one's personal dignity. Antiimperial and anticolonial movements thus came to be endowed with genuine political passion.

It is revealing to contemplate Figure 8, which shows how the longevity of empires has shrunk dramatically of late. More importantly, it suggests that in our time the exercise of international influence is likely to be both too costly and eventually counterproductive, if it comes to be seen by others as involving a reversion to imperial domination. Therein lies an important lesson for the world's currently dominant power: the only way to exercise leadership is through subtle indirection and consensual rule. America's model is neither the Roman nor the British empire; perhaps in the future the Chinese may draw a more relevant lesson from their imperial past of how a deferential tributary system can work.

In any case, the combined impact of global political awakening and modern technology contributes to the acceleration of political history. What once took centuries now takes a decade; what took a decade now happens in a single year. The paramountcy of any power will henceforth come under mounting pressure for adaptation, alteration, and eventual abolition. The dynamism of a populist–nationalist awakening on every continent involving the empowerment of the hitherto largely passive majority of humanity signals not only that traditional

FIGURE 8 ❖ DECLINING IMPERIAL LONGEVITY

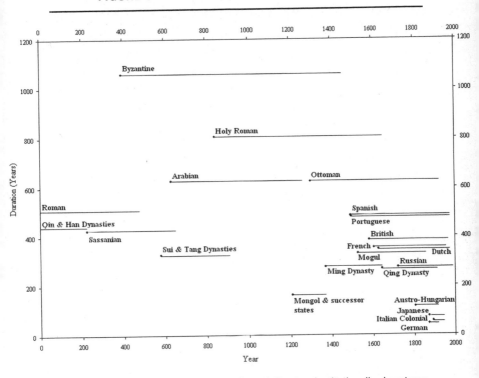

This figure lists major examples of empires, defined as institutionalized systems of rule over multilingual and multiethnic communities by administrators capable of understanding and implementing written instructions from the center. The chart does not include short-lived empires of conquest dependent on the survival of the conqueror. An empire's beginning is coincidental with the first major expansion of rule over an alien population; its end is coincidental with the loss of most foreign dominions.

Prepared by Thomas Williams and Brett Edkins

empires have seen their day but that heavy-handed global domination by a single state will not historically endure.

Global systemic instability, moreover, is likely to be prompted in many parts of the world by challenges to existing state frontiers. In Asia and Africa especially, state borders are often imperial legacies and do not reflect ethnic or linguistic boundaries. These borders are vulnerable to increased pressure as heightened political consciousness leads to more assertive territorial aspirations. In the longer run, even the Sino–Russian border may prove untenable given the drastically uneven demographics of the Far East.

The largely anti-Western character of populist activism has less to do with ideological or religious bias and more with historical experience. Western (or European) domination is part of the living memory of hundreds of millions of Asians and Africans, and of some Latin Americans (though in this case its sharp edge is pointed at the United States). That memory may be vague, even factually wrong, but it is part of the historical lore that defines the political content of the new self-awareness. In the vast majority of states, national identity and national emancipation are associated with the end of foreign imperial domination, an ending often portrayed in heroic epics of selfless sacrifice. This is as true in such large and increasingly self-confident states as India or China as it is in Congo or Haiti.

Anti-Westernism is thus more than a populist attitude. It is an integral part of the shifting global demographic, economic, and political balance. Not only does the non-Western population already far outnumber the Euro-Atlantic world (by 2020, Europe and North America are likely to account for only 15 percent of the world population), but the non-West's awakened political aspirations generate significant momentum for the ongoing redistribution of power. The resentments, emotions, and quest for status of billions are a qualitatively new factor of power.

The power shift is most evident in the increased economic power of the Asian states. Whatever the exact prospects for China, Japan, India, and South Korea—as well as Indonesia, Pakistan, and Iran—most of them will soon rank with the European states as the world's most dynamic and expanding economies. Add in Brazil, Mexico, and perhaps some other non-Asian states, and it is no wonder that Western-dominated global financial institutions such as the World Bank, the IMF, and the WTO are coming under increased pressure to redistribute existing decision-making arrangements.

East Asia will likely be the next region to define its economic and political interests on a transnational basis, either with China at the helm of an East Asian community and Japan somewhat marginalized, or (less likely) with China and Japan managing to contrive some form of partnership. (The Japanese, seeking to dilute China's preeminence, have been pressing to open membership in the emerging Asian community to the United States and Australia.) But even the narrower version of such a grouping would represent a major change in world affairs and a significant reduction of the Euro-Atlantic world's traditional dominance. In effect, a tripartite division of the United States, the European Union, and East Asia is emerging, with India, Russia, Brazil, and perhaps Japan preferring to act as swing states according to their national interests. Russia's residual resentment of

FIGURE 9 ❖ GLOBAL POPULATION, 2005

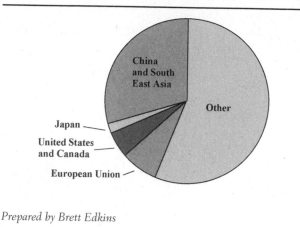

Prepared by Brett Edkins

America's special status may tempt Moscow to associate itself with America's rising rivals.

At some point we could see the emergence of a more pointedly anti-U.S. coalition led by China in East Asia and by India
and Russia in Eurasia. It could then draw in Iran. Although
that may seem far-fetched now, it is noteworthy that after the
first ever Chinese–Indian–Russian summit in St. Petersburg
in the summer of 2006, some Chinese foreign affairs special-
ists wrote nostalgically that Lenin had once advocated an
anti-Western alliance among these three countries. They
pointedly noted that such an alliance would embrace 40 percent of the world's people, 44 percent of its surface, and 22
percent of its GNP.

In this increasingly complicated global context, much will
depend on whether America succeeds in restoring some degree of comity in its relations with the world of Islam. A pro-

FIGURE 10

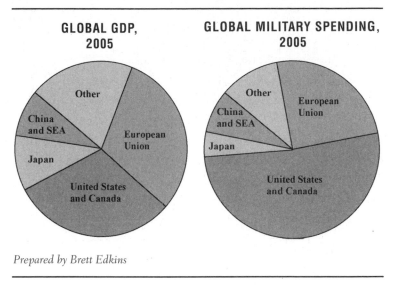

GLOBAL GDP,
2005

GLOBAL MILITARY SPENDING,
2005

Prepared by Brett Edkins

tracted failure to do so will create opportunities for China to enhance its role, not only with Indonesia or Pakistan but also with Iran and the Persian Gulf states. If America's position in the region continues to deteriorate, a Chinese political presence might be very welcome. That would greatly increase China's global influence and could even tempt some European states to conclude that it is in the long-term interest of the European Union to forge a special relationship with the energetically emerging East Asian community.

Given America's growing global indebtedness (it now borrows some 80 percent of the world's savings) and huge trade deficits, a major financial crisis, especially in an atmosphere of emotionally charged and globally pervasive anti-American feeling, could have dire consequences for America's well-being and security. The euro is becoming a serious rival to the dollar and there is talk of an Asian counterpart to both. A hostile Asia and a self-absorbed Europe could at some point become less inclined to continue financing the U.S. debt.

For the United States, several geopolitical conclusions thus follow. First, it is essential for America to preserve and fortify its special transatlantic ties. The United States needs a politically purposeful Europe as a global partner. But while America needs Europe's help in formulating a globally responsible policy, Europe needs America even more. Otherwise it could lapse into self-centered and divisive nationalism, devoid of a larger global mission. If Turkey and Ukraine become convinced that the road to Europe is closed to them, the former may slide into the restless and religiously stirring Middle East, while the latter's vulnerability will excite Russia's residual imperial ambitions.

However, because the new global political realities are pointing to a decline in traditional Western domination, the Atlantic community must become open to as much participation by successful non-Western states as is feasible. That means, first and foremost, a serious effort to engage Japan (and, by extension, South Korea) in expanded participation in key transatlantic consultations. It should also involve a special role for Japan in expanded NATO security planning as well as voluntary participation in some NATO missions. In brief, by selectively drawing the more advanced and democratic non-European states into closer collaboration on global issues, a dominant core of moderation, wealth, and democracy can continue to project a constructive worldwide influence.

It is almost a certainty that Japan before long will shed its pacifist stance—an understandable reaction to the horrors of Hiroshima and Nagasaki, subsequently enshrined in its America-produced constitution—and assume a more self-reliant security role. In doing so, Japan will inevitably become a significant military power. Its involvement in NATO's command exercises and in some of its peacekeeping missions would pose less of a hostile challenge to China than a Japan that is perceived in Beijing either as primarily extending the American military presence in the Far East or as increasingly engaged in a solitary buildup of its national power.

America has also an interest in promoting Sino-Japanese reconciliation, for that will help to engage China in the larger global system while reducing the prospects of a potentially dangerous Sino-Japanese rivalry. Though a Japan closely associated with the West is in America's interest, it does not follow that hostility between Japan and China is beneficial to either America or East Asia. Conversely, it is unlikely that Chinese–Japanese reconciliation would result in Japan becoming seduced by the notion of an East Asian community in which China essentially dominates the mainland and from which America is increasingly excluded. Engagement with China, alliance with Japan, and stable Chinese–Japanese accommodation are therefore mutually reinforcing.

The Chinese are both patient and calculating. That gives America and Japan, as well as an enlarging Atlantic community, time to engage China in shared responsibility for global leadership. In the years to come, China will either be a key player in a more genuinely fair global system or the principal threat to that system's stability, either because of a domestic crisis or some external challenge. Accordingly, the United States should encourage an increased role for China in various international institutions and undertakings.

It is time to face the fact that the G8 summit of "world leaders" has become an anachronism. Contrary to claims, its membership represents neither the most advanced economies nor genuine democracies. Russia's participation satisfies neither of these criteria, while the absence of China as well as India, Brazil, Indonesia, and South Africa, shows that the G8 has become a relic that should give way to a new arrangement. A new annual consultative summit should bring together the key political and economic powers for a much-needed dialogue about global conditions and trends. Given Beijing's absence from the G8, the United States should consult especially with China regarding the membership and agenda for a more ambitious initiative.

A more representative body—even if still informal and outside the U.N. system—could address, in a way more in keeping with the spirit of the times, such basic issues as equity in nuclear nonproliferation, the proper division of burdens in alleviating global poverty, or the common need of rich and poor countries to face the implications of global warming. G8 discussions of these issues today are conducted within historically anachronistic confines.

Even with this new institution, it will still behoove America to infuse a sense of common direction into the restless globe. America is, and will remain for some time, the only power with the potential for moving the global community in the needed direction. But its ability to do that may require something like a national epiphany best summarized (though at the risk of some overstatement) by two notorious phrases: cultural revolution and regime change. The fact is that both America and American policy need a renewal derived from the American people's appreciation of the revolutionary impact of a politically more assertive humanity.

The basic requirements of global leadership are now vastly different from what they were during the British empire. No longer is military power, reinforced by economic prowess and exercised by a superior elite pursuing a sophisticated strategy, sufficient to sustain imperial domination. In the past, power to control exceeded power to destroy. It took less effort and cost to govern a million people than to kill a million people.

Today the opposite is true: power to destroy exceeds the power to control. And the means of destruction are becoming more accessible to more actors, both states and political movements. Consequently, with absolute security for a few (notably America itself) becoming only relative security for all, collective vulnerability puts a premium on intelligent, cooperative governance, reinforced by power that is viewed as legitimate. Global leadership now must be accompanied by a social consciousness, a readiness to compromise regarding some aspects of one's own sovereignty, a cultural appeal with more than just hedonistic content, and a genuine respect for the diversity of human traditions and values.

At the onset of the global era, a dominant power has therefore no choice but to pursue a foreign policy that is truly globalist in spirit, content, and scope. Nothing could be worse for America, and eventually the world, than if American policy were universally viewed as arrogantly imperial in a postimperial age, mired in a colonial relapse in a postcolonial time, selfishly indifferent in the face of unprecedented global interdependence, and culturally self-righteous in a religiously diverse world. The crisis of American superpower would then become terminal.

It is essential that America's second chance after 2008 be more successful than the first *for there will be no third chance.* America urgently needs to fashion a truly post–Cold War globalist foreign policy. It still can do so, provided the next president, aware that "the strength of a great power is diminished if it ceases to serve an idea," tangibly relates American power to the aspirations of politically awakened humanity.

Afterthoughts on Iraq and the War on Terror

Senate Foreign Relations Committee Testimony
Zbigniew Brzezinski, February 1, 2007

Mr. Chairman:

Your hearings come at a critical juncture in the U.S. war of choice in Iraq, and I commend you and Senator Lugar for scheduling them.

It is time for the White House to come to terms with two central realities:

1. The war in Iraq is a historic, strategic, and moral calamity. Undertaken under false assumptions, it is undermining America's global legitimacy. Its collateral civilian casualties as well as some abuses are tarnishing America's moral credentials. Driven by Manichean impulses and imperial hubris, it is intensifying regional instability.

2. Only a political strategy that is historically relevant rather than reminiscent of colonial tutelage can provide the needed framework for a tolerable resolution of both the war in Iraq and the intensifying regional tensions.

If the United States continues to be bogged down in a protracted bloody involvement in Iraq, *the final destination on this downhill track is likely to be a head-on conflict with Iran and with much of the world of Islam at large.* A plausible scenario for a military collision with Iran involves Iraqi failure to meet the benchmarks; followed by accusations of Iranian responsibility for the failure; then by some provocation in Iraq or a terrorist act in the U.S. blamed on Iran; culminating in a "defensive" U.S. military action against Iran that plunges a lonely America into a spreading and deepening quagmire eventually ranging across Iraq, Iran, Afghanistan, and Pakistan.

A mythical historical narrative to justify the case for such a protracted and potentially expanding war is already being articulated. Initially justified by false claims about WMDs in Iraq, the war is now being redefined as the "decisive ideological struggle" of our time, reminiscent of the earlier collisions with Nazism and Stalinism. In that context, Islamist extremism and al Qaeda are presented as the equivalents of the threat posed by Nazi Germany and then Soviet Russia, and 9/11 as the equivalent of the Pearl Harbor attack which precipitated America's involvement in World War II.

This simplistic and demagogic narrative overlooks the fact that Nazism was based on the military power of the industrially most advanced European state; and that Stalinism was able to mobilize not only the resources of the victorious and militarily powerful Soviet Union but also had worldwide appeal through its Marxist doctrine. In contrast, most Muslims are not embracing Islamic fundamentalism; al Qaeda is an isolated fundamentalist Islamist aberration; most Iraqis are engaged in strife because the American occupation of Iraq destroyed the Iraqi state; while Iran—though gaining in regional influence—is itself politically divided, economically and militarily weak. To argue that America is already at war in the region with a wider Islamic threat, of which Iran is the epicenter, is to promote a self-fulfilling prophecy.

Deplorably, the Administration's foreign policy in the Middle East region has lately relied almost entirely on such sloganeering. Vague and inflammatory talk about "a new strategic context" which is based on "clarity" and which prompts "the birth pangs of a new Middle East" is breeding intensifying anti-Americanism and is increasing the danger of a long-term collision between the United States and the Islamic world. Those in charge of U.S. diplomacy have also adopted a posture of moralistic self-ostracism toward Iran strongly reminiscent of John Foster Dulles's attitude of the early 1950s toward Chinese Communist leaders (resulting among other things in the well-known episode of the refused handshake). It took some two decades and a half before another Republican president was finally able to undo that legacy.

One should note here also that practically no country in the world shares the Manichean delusions that the Administration so passionately articulates. The result is growing political isolation of, and pervasive popular antagonism toward the U.S. global posture.

*   *   *

It is obvious by now that the American national interest calls for a significant change of direction. There is in fact a dominant consensus in favor of a change: American public opinion now holds that the war was a mistake; that it should not be escalated, that a regional political process should be explored; and that an Israeli-Palestinian accommodation is an essential element of the needed policy alteration and should be actively pursued. It is noteworthy that profound reservations regarding the Administration's policy have been voiced by a number of leading Republicans. One need only invoke here the expressed views of the much admired President Gerald Ford, former Secretary of State James Baker, former National Security Adviser Brent Scowcroft and several leading Republican senators, John Warner, Chuck Hagel, and Gordon Smith among others.

The urgent need today is for a strategy that seeks to create a political framework for a resolution of the problems posed both by the US occupation of Iraq and by the ensuing civil and sectarian conflict. Ending the occupation and shaping a regional security dialogue should be the mutually reinforcing goals of such a strategy, but both goals will take time and require a genuinely serious U.S. commitment.

The quest for a political solution for the growing chaos in Iraq should involve four steps:

1. *The United States should reaffirm explicitly and unambiguously its determination to leave Iraq in a reasonably short period of time.*

Ambiguity regarding the duration of the occupation in fact encourages unwillingness to compromise and intensifies the on-going civil strife. Moreover, such a public declaration is needed to allay fears in the Middle East of a new and enduring American imperial hegemony. Right or wrong, many view the establishment of such a hegemony as the primary reason for the American intervention in a region only recently free of colonial domination. That perception should be discredited from the highest U.S. level. Perhaps the U.S. Congress could do so by a joint resolution.

> 2. *The United States should announce that it is undertaking talks with the Iraqi leaders to jointly set with them a date by which U.S. military disengagement should be completed, and the resulting setting of such a date should be announced as a joint decision. In the meantime, the U.S. should avoid military escalation.*

It is necessary to engage all Iraqi leaders—including those who do not reside within "the Green Zone"—in a serious discussion regarding the proposed and jointly defined date for U.S. military disengagement because the very dialogue itself will help identify the authentic Iraqi leaders with the self-confidence and capacity to stand on their own legs without U.S. military protection. Only Iraqi leaders who can exercise real power beyond "the Green Zone" can eventually reach a genuine Iraqi accommodation. The painful reality is that much of the current Iraqi regime, characterized by the Bush administration as "representative of the Iraqi people," defines itself largely by its physical location: the four square miles–large U.S. fortress within Baghdad, protected by a wall in places fifteen feet thick, manned by heavily armed U.S. military, popularly known as "the Green Zone."

3. *The United States should issue jointly with appropriate Iraqi leaders, or perhaps let the Iraqi leaders issue, an invitation to all neighbors of Iraq (and perhaps some other Muslim countries such as Egypt, Morocco, Algeria, and Pakistan) to engage in a dialogue regarding how best to enhance stability in Iraq in conjunction with U.S. military disengagement and to participate eventually in a conference regarding regional stability.*

The United States and the Iraqi leadership need to engage Iraq's neighbors in serious discussion regarding the region's security problems, but such discussions cannot be undertaken while the U.S. is perceived as an occupier for an indefinite duration. Iran and Syria have no reason to help the United States consolidate a permanent regional hegemony. It is ironic, however, that both Iran and Syria have lately called for a regional dialogue, exploiting thereby the self-defeating character of the largely passive—and mainly sloganeering—U.S. diplomacy.

A serious regional dialogue promoted directly or indirectly by the U.S., could be buttressed at some point by a wider circle of consultations involving other powers with a stake in the region's stability, such as the EU, China, Japan, India, and Russia. Members of this Committee might consider exploring informally with the states mentioned their potential interest in such a wider dialogue.

4. *Concurrently, the United States should activate a credible and energetic effort to finally reach an Israeli-Palestinian peace, making it clear in the process as to what the basic parameters of such a final accommodation ought to involve.*

The United States needs to convince the region that the U.S. is committed both to Israel's enduring security and to fairness for the Palestinians who have waited for more than forty years now for their own separate state. Only an external and activist intervention can promote the long-delayed settlement for the record shows that the Israelis and the Palestinians will never do so on their own. Without such a settlement, both nationalist and fundamentalist passions in the region will in the longer run doom any Arab regime which is perceived as supportive of U.S. regional hegemony.

After World War II, the United States prevailed in the defense of democracy in Europe because it successfully pursued a long-term political strategy of uniting its friends and dividing its enemies, of soberly deterring aggression without initiating hostilities, all the while also exploring the possibility of negotiated arrangements. Today, America's global leadership is being tested in the Middle East. A similarly wise strategy of genuinely constructive political engagement is now urgently needed.

It is also time for the Congress to assert itself.

Terrorized by "War on Terror": How a Three-Word Mantra Has Undermined America

Washington Post Op-Ed
March 25, 2007

The "war on terror" has created a culture of fear in America. The Bush administration's elevation of these three words into a national mantra since the horrific events of 9/11 has had a pernicious impact on American democracy, on America's psyche and on U.S. standing in the world. Using this phrase has actually undermined our ability to effectively confront the real challenges we face from fanatics who may use terrorism against us.

The damage these three words have done—a classic self-inflicted wound—is infinitely greater than any wild dreams entertained by the fanatical perpetrators of the 9/11 attacks when they were plotting against us in distant Afghan caves. The phrase itself is meaningless. It defines neither a geographic context nor our presumed enemies. Terrorism is not an enemy but a technique of warfare—political intimidation through the killing of unarmed non-combatants.

But the little secret here may be that the vagueness of the phrase was deliberately (or instinctively) calculated by its sponsors. Constant reference to a "war on terror" did accomplish one major objective: It stimulated the emergence of a culture of fear. Fear obscures reason, intensifies emotions, and makes it easier for demagogic politicians to mobilize the public on behalf of the policies they want to pursue. The war of choice in Iraq could never have gained the congressional support it got without the psychological linkage between the shock of 9/11 and the postulated existence of Iraqi weapons of mass destruction. Support for President Bush in the 2004 elections was also mobilized in part by the notion that "a nation at war" does not change its commander in chief in midstream. The sense of a pervasive but otherwise imprecise danger was thus channeled in a politically expedient direction by the mobilizing appeal of being "at war."

To justify the "war on terror," the administration has lately crafted a false historical narrative that could even become a self-fulfilling prophecy. By claiming that its war is similar to earlier U.S. struggles against Nazism and then Stalinism (while ignoring the fact that both Nazi Germany and Soviet Russia were first-rate military powers, a status al Qaeda neither has nor can achieve), the administration could be preparing the case for war with Iran. Such war would then plunge America into a protracted conflict spanning Iraq, Iran, Afghanistan, and perhaps also Pakistan.

The culture of fear is like a genie that has been let out of its bottle. It acquires a life of its own—and can become demoralizing. America today is not the self-confident and determined nation that responded to Pearl Harbor; nor is it the America that heard from its leader, at another moment of crisis, the powerful words "the only thing we have to fear is fear itself"; nor is it the calm America that waged the Cold War with quiet persistence despite the knowledge that a real war could be initiated abruptly within minutes and prompt the death of 100 million Americans within just a few hours. We are now divided, uncertain and potentially very susceptible to panic in the event of another terrorist act in the United States itself.

That is the result of five years of almost continuous national brainwashing on the subject of terror, quite unlike the more muted reactions of several other nations (Britain, Spain, Italy, Germany, Japan, to mention just a few) that also have suffered painful terrorist acts. In his latest justification for his war in Iraq, President Bush even claims absurdly that he has to continue waging it lest al Qaeda cross the Atlantic to launch a war of terror here in the United States.

Such fear-mongering, reinforced by security entrepreneurs, the mass media and the entertainment industry, generates its own momentum. The terror entrepreneurs, usually described as experts on terrorism, are necessarily engaged in competition to justify their existence. Hence their task is to convince the public that it faces new threats. That puts a premium on the presentation of credible scenarios of ever-more-horrifying acts of violence, sometimes even with blueprints for their implementation.

That America has become insecure and more paranoid is hardly debatable. A recent study reported that in 2003, Congress identified 160 sites as potentially important national targets for would-be terrorists. With lobbyists weighing in, by the end of that year the list had grown to 1,849; by the end of 2004, to 28,360; by 2005, to 77,769. The national database of possible targets now has some 300,000 items in it, including the Sears Tower in Chicago and an Illinois Apple and Pork Festival.

Just last week, here in Washington, on my way to visit a journalistic office, I had to pass through one of the absurd "security checks" that have proliferated in almost all the privately owned office buildings in this capital—and in New York City. A uniformed guard required me to fill out a form, show an I.D., and in this case explain in writing the purpose of my visit. Would a visiting terrorist indicate in writing that the purpose is "to blow up the building"? Would the guard be able to arrest such a self-confessing, would-be suicide bomber? To make matters more absurd, large department stores, with their crowds of shoppers, do not have any comparable procedures. Nor do concert halls or movie theaters. Yet such "security" procedures have become routine, wasting hundreds of millions of dollars and further contributing to a siege mentality.

Government at every level has stimulated the paranoia. Consider, for example, the electronic billboards over interstate highways urging motorists to "Report Suspicious Activity" (drivers in turbans?). Some mass media have made their own contribution. The cable channels and some print media have found that horror scenarios attract audiences, while terror "experts" as "consultants" provide authenticity for the apocalyptic visions fed to the American public. Hence the proliferation of programs with bearded "terrorists" as the central villains. Their general effect is to reinforce the sense of the unknown but lurking danger that is said to increasingly threaten the lives of all Americans.

The entertainment industry has also jumped into the act. Hence the TV serials and films in which the evil characters have recognizable Arab features, sometimes highlighted by religious gestures that exploit public anxiety and stimulate Islamophobia. Arab facial stereotypes, particularly in newspaper cartoons, have at times been rendered in a manner sadly reminiscent of the

Nazi anti-Semitic campaigns. Lately, even some college student organizations have become involved in such propagation, apparently oblivious to the menacing connection between the stimulation of racial and religious hatreds and the unleashing of the unprecedented crimes of the Holocaust.

The atmosphere generated by the "war on terror" has encouraged legal and political harassment of Arab Americans (generally loyal Americans) for conduct that has not been unique to them. A case in point is the reported harassment of the Council on American-Islamic Relations (CAIR) for its attempts to emulate, not very successfully, the American Israel Public Affairs Committee (AIPAC). Some House Republicans recently described CAIR members as "terrorist apologists" who should not be allowed to use a Capitol meeting room for a panel discussion.

Social discrimination, for example toward Muslim air travelers, has also been its unintended byproduct. Not surprisingly, animus toward the United States even among Muslims otherwise not particularly concerned with the Middle East has intensified, while America's reputation as a leader in fostering constructive interracial and interreligious relations has suffered egregiously.

The record is even more troubling in the general area of civil rights. The culture of fear has bred intolerance, suspicion of foreigners, and the adoption of legal procedures that undermine fundamental notions of justice. Innocent until proven guilty has been diluted if not undone, with some—even U.S. citizens—incarcerated for lengthy periods of time without effective and prompt access to due process. There is no known, hard evidence that such excess has prevented significant acts of terrorism, and convictions for would-be terrorists of any kind have been few and far between. Someday Americans will be as ashamed of this record as they now have become of the earlier instances in U.S. history of panic by the many prompting intolerance against the few.

In the meantime, the "war on terror" has gravely damaged the United States internationally. For Muslims, the similarity between the rough treatment of Iraqi civilians by the U.S. military and of the Palestinians by the Israelis has prompted a widespread sense of hostility toward the United States in general. It's not the "war on terror" that angers Muslims watching the news on television, it's the victimization of Arab civilians. And the resentment is not limited to Muslims. A recent BBC poll of 28,000 people in 27 countries that sought respondents' assessments of the role of states in international affairs resulted in Israel, Iran, and the United States being rated (in that order) as the states with "the most negative influence on the world." Alas, for some that is the new axis of evil!

The events of 9/11 could have resulted in a truly global solidarity against extremism and terrorism. A global alliance of moderates, including Muslim ones, engaged in a deliberate campaign both to extirpate the specific terrorist networks and to terminate the political conflicts that spawn terrorism would have been more productive than a demagogically proclaimed and largely solitary U.S. "war on terror" against "Islamo-fascism." Only a confidently determined and reasonable America can promote genuine international security which then leaves no political space for terrorism.

Acknowledgments

Traditionally authors acknowledge the help received in writing a book. I do so with pleasure, though I believe that brevity is not incompatible with respect for the tradition. So I will be brief.

The Center for Strategic and International Studies (CSIS) has been my intellectual home for the past quarter century. I have benefited from its spirit of bipartisanship and creative blend of strategy, diplomacy, and economics, as well as its unique mix of scholarship and practical involvement in key policy issues.

For more than a decade I have chaired a semimonthly Current Issues luncheon at the Foreign Policy Institute of the School for Advanced International Studies at Johns Hopkins University. The luncheon's diverse membership has provided a perfect setting for a continuing review of the most salient current issues that America confronts.

Candice Wessling, my special assistant at CSIS, has been remarkably effective in imposing a reliable but also congenial order on my various activities, thereby making it possible for me to concentrate on writing this book.

Thomas Williams, my research assistant while I wrote the book, and Brett Edkins, his successor in the final stages of preparation for publication, provided critical support for this undertaking. Tom prepared in meticulous detail the research papers on which I drew in writing this book and he also suggested some important additional lines of inquiry. Brett developed most of the charts and he as well as Tom carefully reviewed my initial drafts. Both, I am convinced, will do well in the years ahead.

William Frucht, my editor, improved my drafts without rewriting them, sharpened my points, encouraged new avenues of investigation—and did all that with respect for my original intent . . . a perfect editor.

Finally, my wife has been patient and encouraging.

ZB

Index

About the Author

ZBIGNIEW BRZEZINSKI, formerly President Jimmy Carter's National Security Advisor, is a counselor and trustee at the Center for Strategic and International Studies and a professor of American foreign policy at the School of Advanced International Studies at Johns Hopkins University. His many books include *The Choice: Global Domination or Global Leadership* and *The Grand Chessboard: American Primacy and Its Geostrategic Imperatives.* He lives in Washington, D.C.